In THE of THE BRONTËS

EDDIE FLINTOFF

COUNTRYSIDE BOOKS
Newbury, Berkshire

Also in this series:
In the Steps of Jane Austen
In the Steps of Thomas Hardy

First Published 1993
© Eddie Flintoff 1993

COUNTRYSIDE BOOKS
3 CATHERINE ROAD
NEWBURY, BERKSHIRE

ISBN 1 85306 230 8

Cover picture of Haworth Moor courtesy of
Bradford Economic Development Unit.

Produced through MRM Associates Ltd., Reading
Printed by J.W. Arrowsmith Ltd., Bristol

Contents

Cumbria

Richmond •

Northallerton •

Kirkby
Lonsdale
• ② Cowan Bridge

North

⑥ Knaresborough •

Harrogate •

Colne • ④ •
⑬ Keighley
⑦ •
Lancashire ⑪ Haworth Leeds •
① Bradford •
⑧ ⑤ ③
Halifax •

Huddersfield •

Area map showing the location of the walks *(not to scale)*

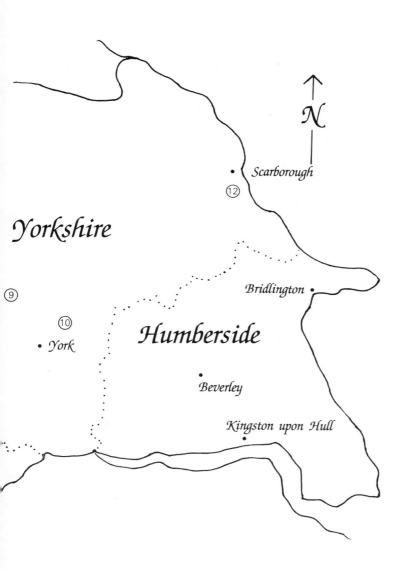

Preface

This book is the first, so far as I know, to visit the various places to which the Brontës went at one time or another and to follow routes actually used by the Brontës themselves. Every ramble in the book contains at least one section which it is as good as certain was used by one or other member of the family, including Patrick and Branwell.

Travelling on foot had been in the blood since before Mr Brontë came to England. When he moved to Yorkshire we have first-hand evidence that he tramped round Dewsbury, Hartshead and Thornton on his parish duties. When the family moved to Haworth, it seems likely that here, too, he visited the remote corners of his sprawling curacy on foot. It was to be the same with the children. Even before they were of an age to go to school we hear of the young teenage servants taking them for walks on the moors. When they reached Cowan Bridge the girls were expected as a matter of course to walk to and from the church at Tunstall on Sundays. By the time Charlotte's friends Mary Taylor and Ellen Nussey were coming over to Haworth to stay, rambles along Sladen Beck to the so-called Brontë Seat, and even perhaps as far as Ponden Kirk, had become a regular event.

Even when the children began to go their separate ways they still retained their love of long walks. Charlotte plainly took strolls with her friends in every direction from the houses at which she stayed in Birstall and Gomersal. And memories of these served to give precision to successive chapters of *Shirley*. Branwell, who plumed himself on the long walks he took, walked everywhere. He walked from Haworth to Roe Head and back, from Broughton-in-Furness to the summit of Black Combe and back, from the same place to Rydal and back along Wordsworth's river Duddon. He certainly went to and from Calderdale on foot both when he worked on the railway and when he was just walking over to

Halifax to see his drinking-friends. Emily confined her walks to the hills around Haworth. Accompanied by her dog, and often carrying a buffet, she tramped the moors to the west of Haworth and Stanbury, probably falling into conversation with the farmers she met on the way. Even in her brief spell at Law Hill she must have explored north into Southowram to have encountered the weird Gothic frontage of High Sunderland Hall and the curiously named farm beyond it. Anne, by contrast, preferred the Vale of York and the sea. A poem written on 30 December 1842 shows that she visited the Long Plantation, a wood near Thorp Green visited on one of our walks, and drawings of Little Ouseburn Church and probably the bridge there, shows she visited them, too. *Agnes Grey* and *The Tenant of Wildfell Hall* prove she had climbed the headland on which Scarborough Castle stood and almost certainly explored the wooded dales and rugged coast to the north of the resort.

This shows that a love of walking was something shared by all the Brontës and I seriously believe that slowly exploring these places on foot – the way the Brontës themselves did – enables one, as no sudden visit by car can, to piece together what it was in each place that evoked such fine creative talent. Some of the places have changed a great deal; but every walk contains some section where time seems to have stood still. And here the perceptive walker can experience for a moment what his great predecessors felt as long ago they too set out:

> 'For the moors! For the moors, where the short grass
>   Like velvet beneath us should lie!
> For the moors! For the moors, where each high pass
>   Rose sunny against the clear sky.'

Good walking!

Eddie Flintoff
May 1993

Calendar

1777– 1800	Birth of Patrick Brontë (then Brunty) at Emdale, Drumbally-roney, Northern Ireland (1777). Maria Branwell born at Penzance (1783). Patrick meets the Rev Andrew Harshaw and begins lessons in the Classics.
1802– 1806	Patrick leaves Ireland for England and enters St John's College, Cambridge (under the name 'Bronte'). He wins various Exhibitions.
1806– 1808	Patrick graduates at Cambridge, is ordained as a Deacon and takes up his curacy at Wethersfield, Essex, where he lodges with Mary Burder's aunt. Friendship with Mary Burder begins.
1809	Patrick leaves Wethersfield amidst some ill-feeling for Wellington, Shropshire. Here he meets William Morgan and John Fennell ('Uncle Fennell'). After nearly 12 months he moves to Dewsbury.
1811– 1814	Patrick moves to Hartshead. Woodhouse Grove School opens with his friend, John Fennell, as First Master. Maria Branwell comes north on a visit and is introduced to Patrick. After a whirlwind romance they marry – in a double wedding with the Morgans – at Guiseley on 29 December 1812. They move to Hightown, where Maria Brontë is born (1814).
1815– 1819	Elizabeth Brontë is born at Hightown. In May 1815 Patrick swaps his curacy at Hartshead for the one at Thornton. Here Charlotte is born (1816), Branwell (1817) and Emily (1818). In 1819 the Rev James Charnock, Perpetual Curate of Haworth, dies. The sensitive task of appointing a successor starts.
1820– 1822	Anne is born at Thornton (1820). Three months later the Brontës move to Haworth. Haworth starts to take its toll. Mrs Brontë falls seriously ill and dies. Elizabeth Branwell, who has come up from Cornwall to look after her sister, stays on at the Parsonage. Mr Brontë proposes marriage to various 'old flames'.
1824– 1825	Cowan Bridge School opens. Maria and Elizabeth are sent there whilst still suffering from the after-effects of whooping cough. Later in the year Charlotte joins them and then Emily. Maria is taken seriously ill and is sent home and dies. Three months later Elizabeth falls ill and is sent home – and dies. The Rev Brontë collects Charlotte and Emily from Silverdale, near Carnforth. They are now all together at home.
1831– 1832	In January 1831 Charlotte goes to Roe Head School where she meets her lifelong friends, Mary Taylor and Ellen Nussey. She

remains at the school until May 1832, when she returns home to teach Emily and Anne.

1834–1836   Branwell begins lessons in painting, completes one (perhaps both) of the two family groups for which he is remembered and contacts the Royal Academy. Charlotte goes back to Roe Head as a teacher (with Emily as a pupil). Branwell makes his abortive journey to London to the Royal Academy. Emily returns home from Roe Head, homesick. Anne takes her place.

1838–1839   Branwell resumes art lessons, takes a studio in Bradford. At some point – perhaps autumn 1838 – Emily goes to Law Hill School near Halifax, where she remains for six months. About the time that she returns Anne goes as governess to Blake Hall and Charlotte to Stone Gappe. Branwell gives up his studio and returns home to receive lessons in the Classics. At the end of the year, after Charlotte has returned from Stone Gappe and Anne from Blake Hall, it is his turn to make ends meet. He sets out for Broughton-in-Furness.

1840   Whilst at Broughton, Branwell contacts Hartley Coleridge about his translations of Horace. He visits him and after some encouragement sends him his translations of *Odes 1*. Under not totally clear circumstances he leaves Broughton and three months later takes up a job on the railway at Sowerby Bridge. By now – from perhaps May – Anne has been teaching at Thorp Green. At the end of the year Hartley Coleridge returns Branwell's translations.

1841   Branwell is promoted to Clerk in Charge at Luddendenfoot Station (on pay not very much less than his father's stipend). In June he sees his first poem in print – in the *Halifax Guardian*.

1842   Mr Brontë takes Charlotte and Emily over to Brussels, where they begin their studies at the Pensionnat Heger. Branwell is sacked for dereliction of duties.

1843   After returning to Haworth for Christmas (1842) with Emily, Charlotte returns to Brussels on her own. Branwell joins Anne at Thorp Green to tutor Edmund Robinson. Mr Brontë pays a visit there in spring time.

1844–1845   Charlotte returns home from Brussels in the New Year of 1844. Anne and Branwell continue at Thorp Green. In May 1845 Arthur Bell Nicholls comes as a curate to Haworth. In the summer of 1845 Anne leaves Thorp Green and – in somewhat mysterious circumstances – Branwell leaves too.

1846–1847   All four Brontë children are at home together producing poems and working on novels. Charlotte sends off the *Poems*, which are published in May 1846. Two copies are sold. The novels, *The Professor*, *Wuthering Heights* and *Agnes Grey*, are sent off and rejections begin. In July 1847 Mr Brontë goes to Manchester for an eye operation and Charlotte begins *Jane Eyre* there. In the summer of 1847 Newby accepts *Wuthering Heights* and *Agnes Grey*. After rejecting *The Professor*, Smith

The Red House at Gomersal, portrayed as Briarmains in Shirley.

Elder and Co accept *Jane Eyre*. All three novels are published by the end of the year.

1848 *The Tenant of Wildfell Hall* is published by Newby. Charlotte and Anne visit London. Tuberculosis attacks the family again. In September Branwell dies; three months later Emily, too; Anne is taken seriously ill.

1849 Anne deteriorates. Charlotte and Ellen take her to Scarborough, where she dies. Charlotte completes *Shirley* and two months later it is published.

1850 By now the identity of Currer Bell is widely known. Charlotte visits London, Edinburgh and Windermere. At the last she is introduced to Mrs Gaskell.

1851– 1852 Charlotte's friendship with George Smith continues. James Taylor also of Smith Elder and Co comes to Haworth to propose before he leaves for Bombay. Mr Brontë makes clear his displeasure at the prospect of Charlotte's marrying. Charlotte starts work on *Villette* (November 1851), which she completes in November 1952. Arthur Bell Nicholls proposes.

1853 *Villette* is published. Arthur Bell Nicholls leaves Haworth. He writes to Charlotte and they start to correspond. From October she starts to see him again. She begins *Emma* (never completed).

1854– **1855**	Charlotte gets engaged to Arthur Bell Nicholls (3 April) and they are married on 29 June. As her father will not attend the wedding she is given away by Miss Wooler (from Roe Head School) and married by a friend of Branwell's, the Rev Sutcliffe Sowden. For their honeymoon they go to Ireland. Following on a walk on the moors late in 1854 Charlotte catches a cold and her health steadily deteriorates. On 31 March 1855 she dies of consumption. Mr Brontë commissions Mrs Gaskell to begin her biography.
1856– **1906**	Mrs Gaskell's *Life of Charlotte Brontë* published (1857) and is followed by a storm of controversy, which leads to a withdrawal from sale of the first edition and some re-writing (see Book List). *The Professor* is published posthumously (1857). Mr Brontë dies (1861) and Arthur Bell Nicholls resigns his curacy and returns to Ireland (1861), where he re-marries (1864). Arthur Bell Nicholls dies (1906).

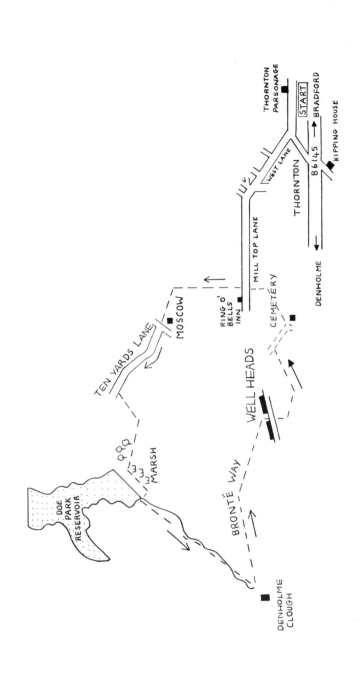

1

Thornton:
The Birthplace of Literary
Genius

Walking Distance: 5 miles

We begin with a look round the village in which Charlotte, Branwell, Emily and Anne were born. We then leave the village by the route by which they moved to Haworth in 1820. From the road we branch off across the fields to explore some of the more picturesque parts of the old 'parish' along routes which it is as good as certain Mr Brontë would have known and used. After a walk along a beautiful secluded valley, we return to Thornton by the Brontë Way.

Although the old village of Thornton itself has now expanded and become little more than a suburb of Bradford, the old 'parish' of Thornton remains surprisingly untouched by the sprawl to the east. Mr Brontë would still recognise the innumerable walled-round fields, the bare green hilltops, the zig-zagging narrow valleys with here and there fresh water marshes, the windswept moorland to the west, the isolated farms, the curious detached lines of weavers' cottages with their mullioned windows, also the dams, the occasional quarries, the panoramic views across England's largest county.

So what was this Thornton 'parish'? Like Haworth it was not actually a parish at all, merely a chapelry within the Parish of Bradford. The Perpetual Curate of Thornton, who was paid a good deal less than the vicar himself – perhaps £155 a year in the case of Thornton – acted as his representative. He conducted the services, taught at Sunday school, visited the sick, performed all the tasks that a full vicar would in this small corner of the huge Bradford parish. I say small,

The village of Thornton. Rev Patrick Brontë took up the incumbency here in 1815.

but in fact even the Thornton chapelry took in a good deal more then than the village of Thornton or the present Parish of Thornton. It also took in Denholme, Clayton, Allerton and Wilsden – much of the countryside in fact to the west of Bradford between Queensbury and the Worth Valley. And we can imagine Mr Brontë, who was a keen walker, ceaselessly walking the tracks and footpaths that formed a grid of routes across his parish.

Mr Brontë took up the incumbency in this remote corner of the Pennines in 1815, as a result of a parochial swap. Mr Brontë, as the Perpetual Curate of Thornton, a Chapelry of Dewsbury, had over time got to know Thomas Atkinson, the Perpetual Curate of Thornton in the Parish of Bradford. With the permission of John Crosse, the Vicar of Bradford, and John Buckworth, the Vicar of Dewsbury, it was agreed that Mr Brontë and Mr Atkinson would exchange livings. Both got something out of it. Mr Atkinson was anxious to live closer to a wealthy young lady, Frances Walker of Lascelles

Hall, to whom a little later he was to get married; Mr Brontë was by contrast to get a substantial rise in remuneration. In Thornton he would receive approximately double what he had at Hartshead. With two young girls already needing an education and a wife expecting a third child this was no small consideration for a man without a private income.

So on May 19, 1815 the Brontës moved into their new home at Thornton, the house in which Charlotte, Branwell, Emily and Anne were all to be born. This at the time was a little smaller than now. It was a pleasant, modest, double-fronted, late Georgian stone building. Just outside the house was a small well from which the servants drew water. Directly in front, was a neat area of walled-off ground at the end of which four steps led up to the front door. Inside the house, the two main rooms, the drawing room and the dressing room, were at either side of the front door. There seems some evidence that the children were born in the room to the right of the front door, the one where there is now an extension. Upstairs there were two bedrooms and as now, in between, a small dressing room where Mr Brontë would wash and shave.

Late in the 19th century some very old people could still remember seeing the family as they went about their business in the village – the girls playing out, presumably in the small garden at the front, Mrs Brontë taking them for walks, the children holding her hand or sometimes in her arms, up one or other of the two or three side streets that then branched off the main street. A Mr Holroyd who lived over at Clayton remembered Mr Brontë going about his parish work over there. 'I remember his figure well, he was a well-built, good-looking man.'

This accessibility obviously brought them into contact with several leading local families. The one about which we know the most was the Firth family of Kipping House. Fortunately the diaries of Elizabeth Firth have survived and are to be seen at Sheffield University Library. These provide a fascinating record of the day to day activities of the Brontë family that is unique, not only for the period at Thornton but Haworth, too.

When Elizabeth was baptised on 26 August 1815 Mr Firth was her godfather and Miss Branwell and Elizabeth Firth, after whom presumably Elizabeth was christened, were the two godmothers. When in years after Mr Brontë and Aunt Branwell mulled over the times at Thornton they thought of them as 'the good old days' with all their social engagements and walks.

But there was more to life at Thornton than that. In addition to his numerous pastoral duties, visits to the sick and dying, weddings and funerals, Mr Brontë was responsible for a restoration of the old Thornton Church, the Bell Chapel, which if it had not been demolished would have given us an opportunity to assess his taste in architecture, etc. Sadly, however, virtually nothing of this curious building now remains – not even adequate written records. All we have are one or two poor photographs and a painting. But we do know that during the long hot summer of 1818 the south side of the chapel was re-faced, the whole of the building re-roofed and a cupola erected. In addition it was redecorated inside and an angel introduced into the interior. Miss Firth noted in her entry for 10 November 1818 the following improbable sounding encounter: 'We went to look at the angel in Thornton Chapel.'

Angels had always been one of Mr Brontë's favourite images. This particular one must have been a painting, probably above the small communion table, executed by a local craftsman and painter, Thomas Driver. (Parish records for 1818 refer to £6 being paid to 'Thomas Driver for painting different things in the chapel'). It seems a pity we cannot now see for ourselves what Mr Brontë's idea of 'beautifying' (his word) the chapel involved.

At least, though, we can turn to the literature he produced at Thornton. For it was whilst he was at Thornton he was at his most creative as a writer. He completed – perhaps even wrote – *The Cottage in the Wood* (1815) and his most

The simple parsonage at Thornton, now a restaurant where Charlotte, Branwell, Emily and Anne were born. The projection at the front of the building is a later addition.

ambitious story, *The Maid of Killarney*. This last, an anonymous work, but certainly by Mr Brontë, is a curious mix of pictures of the old Ireland and Mr Brontë's own political and moral reflections. The precedent provided by these works could only have acted as a spur to the young Brontës.

Contrary to what is often assumed, links were not instantly severed with Thornton when the Brontës left. Elizabeth Firth's diary shows that during 1820 and 1821 Mr Brontë continued to visit the Firths and when Mr Firth fell ill and later died he came to see his old friend and stayed on several days after the funeral. Similarly when almost immediately afterwards Mrs Brontë fell ill, Elizabeth Firth went over to Haworth to see her and on one occasion took Maria and Elizabeth back to Thornton with her. Indeed there is evidence that during 1821 Elizabeth Firth actually sent over one or two sums of money to help her old friends out. And the Firths were not the only family from Thornton who did their bit for the Brontës. There is some evidence that after Mr Brontë had collected Charlotte and Emily from Silverdale following the Cowan Bridge catastrophe, Charlotte was sent to stay for a while with the Down family at Allerton Hall in Mr Brontë's old parish. A letter from a member of the family published many years later records seeing Charlotte in a large four-poster bed wearing a night cap and adds that she often went there.

In view of the word 'often', it is intriguing that one of the characters in Charlotte and Branwell's juvenilia is a General Thornton, a true blue Tory who speaks broad Yorkshire and is described as an 'honest honest man'. With Charlotte's acknowledged tendency to base so many of her characters on people she knew, it is very tempting to see this homely figure as a real person in Thornton and his home, the 'Thornton Hotel', as some house at which the children stayed. The obvious choice must be the Firths who were both friends of Mr Brontë and godparents to the children, too. If this is so, then Thornton Hotel would have been Kipping House. But this is speculative. What I think is sure is that it must have been a wrench leaving Thornton. Somehow I doubt if Mr Brontë was ever to be as carefree and fulfilled again.

THE WALK AROUND THORNTON PARISH

There is some parking on two small car parks to the north and south of Market Street in the middle of Thornton. Access is only possible from the Bradford side of Thornton. If these are full, you can park without difficulty on West Lane.

Wherever you have parked, walk east along Market Street. This narrow lane was the only road to Bradford in the time of the Brontës. Although there were not as many houses then, this was where the pub landlords, butcher, general dealer etc would have plied their trades. In this parish, unlike Haworth, the parson lived at the busy heart of his parish.

On the left you will soon come to the old Parsonage, now a restaurant. The building has not altered greatly since the time of the Brontës, but a small neat extension has been added at the front obliterating the front door and a large ground floor window. To the left and right of the front door stood the drawing room and the dining room. Between the two bedrooms still visible upstairs was a small chamber used as a toilet room. This was where Mr Brontë was standing shaving in the window on a Sunday when he was spotted by a passing Dissenter. In the late 19th century, older inhabitants remembered seeing the children playing out in the street in front of the Parsonage.

Walk further down and you will soon see the nonconformist Kipping Chapel standing on the opposite side of the road to the Parsonage. Although the present building only dates from 1849, there has been a chapel on this site since 1769. This was one of the more important Dissenting chapels even in this hotbed of nonconformity. Despite the slightly confrontational position of the chapel and the parsonage – the chapel came first, incidentally – Mr Brontë seems to have lived in harmony with the two nonconformist ministers there during his time, Mr Calvert and Mr Pool, as well as their flocks. Opposite the chapel you will see Sapgate Lane, one of the few side streets that existed in the time of the Brontës. Both Sapgate Lane and Market Street ahead have properties dating from the time of the Brontës.

Now turn back and walk towards the west end of the old village. On the left you will pass Kipping School (1819). When you reach the triangular shaped fork in the road you will see the Black Horse inn ahead. In the time of the Brontës no fewer than three pubs offered their wares here. In addition to the Black Horse there was the White Horse on the site of the present post office in Kipping Lane and the Bull's Head which occupied much of the present triangle. The pubs were all together at one end of the village; the places of worship at the other!

At the fork turn left down Kipping Lane and cross Thornton Road, which did not exist in the time of the Brontës, to the continuation of Kipping Lane. The barn situated a few yards down on the left provided an illegal meeting place for

Kipping House, home of the Firth family, friends of the Brontës. Elizabeth and Maria stayed here for a time when Mrs Brontë was unwell.

nonconformists to worship in the early 18th century. It was from here that they moved to Kipping Chapel. Past the barn the next house on the left is Kipping House. Here Elizabeth Firth lived, who was a close friend of the Brontës and whose diaries provide us with a detailed picture of life in Thornton during the time Mr Brontë was parson here.

Now turn back uphill, cross Thornton Road and at the fork in the middle of the village walk left up West Lane. It was along this road and Hilltop Lane that the Brontës made their journeys between Thornton and Haworth. Follow the road uphill past the factory on the left. When you meet James Street turn right and 20 yards later fork left up Hill Top Road. The right hand pavement is best. Follow this road for about ⅓ mile. Just before the Ring o' Bells pub on the right and opposite a gravel drive, turn right down a grassy track. Walk ahead to a stile. Through the stile walk ahead keeping close to the wall on the right hand side to another stile. Now walk along a short length of enclosed pathway through another stile to a stile that takes you into a field. Follow the left hand wall to a further stile. Here turn left and walk alongside the wall on your left to another stile. Through this stile keep close to the wallside and walk to a further stile. Pass through this and walk in front of a line of houses to the road.

Turn left and almost immediately right down Ten Yards Lane. Walk for about ¼ mile past Spring Hall Farm. After going round a slight corner look for a stile on your left in the corner of its field. You may see the vandalised public footpath sign lying by it in the grass. Cross this stile and, following the left hand wall, walk downhill. The community visible on the hilltop ahead is Denholme which was a part of Mr Brontë's 'parish'. When you reach the bottom of the hill you will find the stile 25 yards to the right of the (somewhat moist) bottom corner of the field. Go through this and follow the clear path above a depression to a stile at the edge of the wood. In the wood follow the clear path to the right of the ravine down to a stile a few yards to the right of the stream. Over this walk ahead alongside a right hand wall. In 50 yards turn left to another stile and follow the flagged path along the right hand wall. The way here may be both wet and slippery. On the other hand this is an outstanding piece of wetland.

Follow the path round to the right, over a footbridge and through a stile. Turn left along the left hand wall into a field. Then keeping right of the beck follow the indistinct path towards the arch ahead. This was under the Great Northern Railway line from Keighley to Queensbury (opened 1884). Through the arch stay on the right hand side of the beck. The path is mostly just visible. Go through two stiles. After the second stile keep to the left hand side of the wall for about 50 yards then cross a stile on your right into a field. Walk ahead across the field towards a line of cottages. After about 150 yards ford the stream – there is a felicitously placed stepping stone – and continue ahead towards the cottages. About 100 yards before the cottages you will see a footpath sign close to an impressive stone wall. Turn left by this along the clear path uphill. When you reach the top and it looks as though you cannot go any further, turn left and follow the wall to a corner. Now turn right with the wall. You will find yourself on a fenced path signposted 'Brontë Way'. Go through a stile and walk straight ahead. Now keeping the wall on your left go through three stiles.

After the third stile aim half right uphill to a stile to the left of the farmhouse visible ahead. Through this stile aim to the right of the farm towards a gate and stile. Enter a lane, turn left for 10 yards and where the lanes divide you will find a stile next to a building and a green gate. Go through this and aim half left for a stile in the middle of the wall ahead. Keep in the same line to another stile about half way along a line of cottages ahead. Keep the same line to yet another stile and now aim for the furthest right hand corner of the field – just beyond the 1980s Georgian style house. Turn right through a short ginnel into the road.

Turn left for about 100 yards past another pleasant line of cottages. Now cross the road to a public footpath sign and walk down the lane. Turn left at the gate and walk above the house to a stile. Now follow the flagged path along the left hand wall. Follow this path through two stiles. The wall should now be on your right. After 30 yards where the path joins a lane, continue ahead. After another 30 yards go through a gateway and continue ahead with the wall now again on your right. Cross the stile in the corner ahead into a walled lane.

Turn right down this lane until you reach a line of cottages on your left. Turn left along the back of these cottages and walk up a flagged path to a kissing gate leading you into Thornton Cemetery. Walk ahead along the metalled lane. After 40 yards branch left uphill on a pleasant broad green path. At the top of the hill turn left by the gate and walk along a short path to Hill Top Road near the Ring o' Bells. Cross the road to the pavement on the far side and turn right. Where Wicken Lane forks off to the left, keep right and same again a few yards later. Opposite High Wicken Close, fork left down West Lane and walk straight downhill into Thornton.

2

Cowan Bridge: The Lowood School of 'Jane Eyre'

Walking Distance: 5½ miles

This walk begins at Cowan Bridge School, the Lowood School of *Jane Eyre*, and then follows as closely as is now practicable the route which the Brontë girls and their fellow pupils would have taken on Sundays to Tunstall Church, the Brocklebridge Church of *Jane Eyre*. The church is usually open and it is possible to climb a ladder and see the room in which the schoolgirls had their lunches (presumably in relays!). From Tunstall we return by the 'exposed and hilly' road by which they returned to school. However, instead of following the A65 down to the school, which would not be especially pleasant, we detour through Leck in order to return by the woods and the stream where Jane Eyre – and Charlotte – spent their happier moments at school.

Everyone knows that Lowood School is a thin disguise for Cowan Bridge School and Mr Brocklehurst for the Rev William Carus Wilson. But how true is this?

The Rev William Carus Wilson was a man of almost incredible energy. A successful publisher of magazines and religious works, his charitable deeds involved founding schools for poor children. In 1823 he conceived the idea which was to result at last in *Jane Eyre* – of founding a school which would be open to the daughters of the many poor clergy to be found across England. Even granted that Carus Wilson was a very rich man and had, if anything, richer connections, it was an incredible gamble. When the school opened there were just two pupils!

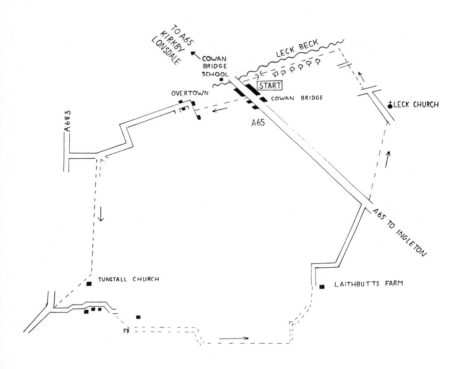

However, the gamble paid off. A year later there were
already 45 girls on the school roll. And with the same drive as
ever Carus Wilson spent even more money, adding a large
two-storey wing (now demolished) at the west end of the
Picards' old property to provide extra teaching and residen-
tial space, and an arcade facing it across the garden (also now
demolished) so that the girls could take some exercise even
when it was raining. All this, the initial purchase of the
property, the furnishing of it and the alterations, he paid for
out of his own pocket, leaving it to the newly appointed
trustees to reimburse him as and when it proved possible.

So, far from Carus Wilson being the cold-blooded figure in
Jane Eyre, he was, with his impulsiveness, an almost Byronic
figure. So what sort of school was it that Maria and Elizabeth
Brontë came to a few months after it had opened on 1 July
1824? The obvious answer must be a school that was still

finding its feet. However, it is clear what the overall ethos was. This was certainly not meant to be a finishing school for fashionable young ladies. It was a school which would provide a highly subsidised, no-nonsense Christian education. The school fees of £14 a year would provide the girl with bed and board and tuition in such subjects as reading, writing and 'cyphering' (arithmetic), as well as grammar, geography, history and needlework. It significantly did not include such lady-like accomplishments as French, music or drawing, for which extra had to be paid. It was the same in clothes. Because these girls came from what the middle classes thought of as poor homes it was stipulated in advance what clothes, etc, the girls should bring to school. Many no doubt made a lot of their clothes themselves. For the 'outer clothing', the school uniform, that is, £3 had to be paid in advance to the school.

Everyday features of school-life have an 'institutional' sound to them. It should not surprise those of us who were away at school or college before the 1950s that there was no

Lowood, the school in Jane Eyre; *an illustration in the 1872 edition by E.M. Wimperis.*

heating in the dormitories. The girls would often rise to find the water in the pitchers frozen. It was the same in many private houses. Nor were meals any better. Breakfast would typically be a bowl of porridge or of bread and milk with a glass of milk; tea in the late afternoon a slice of dry bread (or on Sunday bread and butter) with milk, tea or coffee; supper an oatcake and a glass of water. The only substantial meal was dinner where the girls first had a pudding, often rice, and then a meat course of hot-pot, a joint or meat pie with (separately served) vegetables. By today's standards it sounds like starvation rations. But again it should be said that very many people lived a good deal worse than this. And two important sources of information about the early life of the Brontës both agree that the Brontës did not get much meat at home.

This then was the school to which Mr Brontë brought Maria and Elizabeth a few months after the school was opened. Charlotte arrived in August – and was only 8 at the time – whilst Emily arrived in November. Mr Brontë stayed overnight on at least two occasions, ate with the children and saw the school in action. Far from being put off by what he saw and heard, he came back with yet more children. If this is not an endorsement of the school I do not know what is.

So how did Cowan Bridge come by its fearsome reputation? Everyone who has had children at any school knows that they will dramatise the mostly rather humdrum life there. Some teachers will be demonised; others almost canonised. And so it is in Charlotte's account of Lowood. Miss Scatcherd becomes the villain of the piece; Miss Temple a paragon. From time immemorial another favourite grouse has been school-dinners. And so we find Charlotte singling out occasions on which burnt porridge was served or recalling that on one occasion 'the dinner was served in two tin-plated vessels, whence rose a strong steam redolent of rancid fat' and that she 'found the mess to consist of indifferent potatoes and strange shreds of rusty meat, mixed and cooked together'.

However, I suspect that the real grievances were of a different character altogether. Underlying the account in *Jane Eyre* is the feeling that it was the sheer rigidity of the routine that was most irksome. A typical weekday timetable would work as follows: 6 o'clock, rising bell; 7–8 religious instruction; 8 breakfast; 9–12 lessons; 12–1 exercise; 1 dinner; 2–5 afternoon lessons; 5 tea (with further study for the older girls in the evening). On Sundays the girls were taken by the teachers to Tunstall Church to hear the Rev Wilson take both morning and evening (that is afternoon) services. After the free and easy, perhaps slightly disorganised, life of the Parsonage, this must have been something of what we now call a 'culture-shock'. And it seems evident from the school's confidential reports in the Admission Register that the staff saw this. 'Maria works badly', we read. 'Elizabeth reads little; writes pretty well; ciphers none. Works very badly. Knows nothing of grammar, geography, history or accomplishments'. 'Charlotte writes indifferently. Ciphers a little, and marks neatly, knows nothing of grammar, geography, history or accomplishments. Altogether clever of her age, but knows nothing systematically.' 'Emily reads very prettily, and works a little'. It does seem, sadly, very likely that, whether Helen Burns is in every precise detail the same as Maria, Charlotte would have seen her sister whom she idealised called to order by her surname, possibly made to stand on a stool, 'labelled' in the way so many schools did then, possibly even physically punished. So, though she was probably never punished herself (and became in fact rather a favourite), her anger at what she had seen continued to rankle, was communicated to friends and family and found, of course, its definitive expression in *Jane Eyre* and the first edition of Mrs Gaskell's *Life*.

This was, I believe, the main single reason for Charlotte's lambasting of the school. However, it did not exactly help that Maria and Elizabeth fell ill and died so soon after entering the school. Here too it is clear that the school was in no way to blame. The records show that they monitored the health of the girls. They had been hesitant about taking

View of the fells from Cowan Bridge – these are the hills to which Charlotte refers in Chapter Nine of Jane Eyre *where she speaks of 'noble summits girding a great hill hollow'.*

Maria and Elizabeth in the first place. Mrs Gaskell's *Life* shows that a doctor regularly visited the school. And girls were regularly withdrawn as soon as they contracted any serious illness. The site, too, of the school was anything but unhealthy. By comparison the mortality rate in Haworth was appalling. And that is certainly where the two girls contracted their consumption. Nor was there at this time any kind of epidemic at the school similar to that described in *Jane Eyre*. In Charlotte's mind, however, the petty discipline, the spartan way of life and the premature deaths of her sisters all fused to create the nightmare of Lowood.

Charlotte possessed an almost photographic memory for visual detail. Rightly she made use of this to add exactitude to the people and places in her writings as she shuffled around people, places and events to form a new whole. So it is that in *Jane Eyre* we see the great 'hill hollow' of Gragareth, the 'blue peaks' far away, the woods and the rocky beck with its 'wild primrose plants'. We re-live the bracing walk to and from Tunstall Church. The lay-out of Cowan Bridge is exactly replicated with its 'two wings', one a dormitory, the other a verandah, facing each other across the garden. The routine and the fees are identical. However, this said, there is no way that Lowood is Cowan Bridge, Jane Eyre Charlotte Brontë, or Mr Brocklehurst the Rev William Carus Wilson. Jane Eyre was of a superior social class to Charlotte Brontë. She arrived in the dead of winter; Charlotte arrived at the height of summer. Lowood was an orphan institution founded by a Naomi Brocklehurst, Cowan Bridge a school for the daughters of impoverished clergymen founded by the Rev Wilson. The Brocklehurst girls were large, elegant young ladies in their late teens; one of the Wilson girls was sick through this period, the others too young. Helen Burns died at school; Maria and Elizabeth Brontë were withdrawn from school and died at home. Nor was there any such epidemic as we have in *Jane Eyre*.

In fact, so far as the Brontës were concerned, the Rev Wilson seems to have behaved rather well. When Elizabeth met with an accident she was nursed by one of the teachers – a Miss Evans – in her bedroom in the main building. Emily was a 'pet nursling'. The school contacted Mr Brontë when both Maria and then Elizabeth fell ill. Elizabeth was escorted all the way home under the supervision of a trusted local lady, a Mrs Hardacre. The very next day Charlotte and Emily were despatched to The Cove, a house of Mr Wilson's on the very edge of Morecambe Bay at Silverdale, which he let those girls who could not return home use as a holiday home during the summer. Even if the books he did leave behind do represent a mode of speech that can at times seem hectoring and insensitive, by most reckonings he seems both an able man and a very humane man.

But such is the power of a great creative writer that, for ever more now, Cowan Bridge will be the school at which Jane Eyre saw her friend Helen Burns die.

THE WALK TO TUNSTALL CHURCH

Drive to Cowan Bridge and in the middle turn off the A65 on the road signposted to Leck. Drive a few yards down this and then turn off to the left to park outside the Village Hall.

Retrace your steps to the A65. Cross carefully and turn right along the pavement. Follow this pavement to the old bridge and use this to cross Leck Beck. The line of cottages beyond the beck is all that remains of Cowan Bridge School. If you go past the drive and look on the side wall of the cottage adjacent to the wall you will see a plaque saying:

> 'Maria Elizabeth Charlotte and Emily Brontë lived here as
> pupils in 1824–5'

What remains is in fact the sleeping accommodation of the school. The wing containing the classrooms, which can be seen in old prints of the school, has been demolished as has the sun lounge which ran along the side of the main road from in front of the school towards the beck. The school itself was transferred to Casterton in 1833, as the plaque on the wall also states.

Retrace your steps over the bridge. There used to be – and still legally is – a footpath on the south side of the beck to Overtown and ultimately Tunstall. It may have been the one taken by the girls to Tunstall Church on a Sunday, but it is too difficult to follow now. So keep straight along the A65 past the buildings on the right until you come to a BT telephone box opposite the Methodist Church. Turn right along the signed footpath between a fence and a wall, cross over a stile into a field and walk across this, keeping the wall to your right. At the end cross another stile into another field. This time aim just a degree or two to the right of straight ahead to a gate and stile. Go through this and keeping the same direction, aim for another gate with a farm and bunga-lows visible beyond it.

Once through this, aim towards the buildings in such a

way that you keep the farm itself to the left and the bunga-
lows to the right. The stile is on your left immediately beyond
the farm and leads into a small gravel track. Follow this
rightwards to the metalled road. You are now in Overtown.
From here onwards it is as good as certain that you will be
following the route taken by the clergy daughters to church.

You now follow this road past several renovated farm-
steads and a vast complex, housing animals, for about a mile.
If some of the details have altered – not entirely for the better
– during the last 170 years, you can still enjoy fine views of
the Luneside hills to the west, the Gragareth massif to the east
and the more distant Bowland Fells to the south. Keep along
the road as it bends first left and then right. At the right time
of year the roadside verges can be very luxuriant with cam-
pion, meadowsweet, vetch and honeysuckle.

Go past the entrance to Parkside Farm and its Greywall
herd on the right to where the road turns right for a second
time. Here two tracks enter the road from the left. Take the
one on the right through a gate and go through an enclosure
(where there is some building going on at the time of writing)
to another gate about 50 yards ahead. Go through this
second gate and along the good clear track past a timber
agricultural building to a third gate. Go through this and,
continuing on the good track with the hedge to the right, aim
for a stone barn. You should now have a good view of
Ingleborough as well as Gragareth to the east.

Just beyond the stone barn you will meet a fourth gate. Go
through this. The good track has now come to an end.
However, follow the hedge on the right until you reach a fifth
(wooden) gate. Continue, with the hedge on the right, to a
sixth gate. Go through this and 20 yards ahead you will see a
stile. Climb over this and make your way through machinery
and tyres to a good gravel surface. Turn left through a gate
and then turn sharp right to enter a farmyard.

Pass through two gates: you will now see a clear track
leading down to a metalled road. Leave the track and strike
half right across the field towards the churchyard. As you

Tunstall Church, the Brocklebridge church of Jane Eyre. *The room above the doorway is where the Brontë girls would eat their lunches when attending church.*

approach it you will see a gate and a stile. This is almost certainly the way the girls would have come to church on a Sunday.

Now you have reached Tunstall Parish Church it is worth looking round it. It is here rather than the much nearer Leck Church that the girls from Cowan Bridge had to walk every Sunday during the time the Brontës were at school. The founder of the school was the Vicar of Tunstall. The church, the third on the site, goes back to at least the 13th century but was rebuilt in about 1415. Since the time of the Brontës the church has seen extensive alterations. In 1826 it was re-roofed. In about 1840 the gallery at the west end of the church in which the girls from Cowan Bridge sat was demolished. In 1907 the plaster on the interior walls was stripped away to reveal the masonry. However, the present seating had already been installed by the time the school was opened. And the tiny room in the tower into which the girls used to retreat to eat their lunches is still visible (though access to it is now by way of a ladder rather than directly from the old gallery).

Having had a good look round the church, set off half left across the churchyard and walk between some cypress trees to a gate. Turn left along a metalled road which soon becomes a stone track. In *Jane Eyre* Charlotte mentions that the girls were led back to Cowan Bridge by a different route from the one by which they had walked to the church; 'an exposed and hilly road' where the wind 'almost flayed the skin' from their faces. The route you are now following is by far the best candidate for this. Go straight along the track. Do not turn left to Churchfield House. After 200 yards you will come to two gates facing each other across the track. Here turn right off the track and then walk half left across the field to a footbridge. Cross this bridge and go left for about 10 yards to join another track. Turn right along this to pass a renovated farm on the left.

Continue along the track through a pleasant wood uphill. When the track ends at two gates take the right hand gate and follow the left hand fence over another hill to a gate in the left hand corner. Go through this and, keeping the fence on your left, go down to another gate, continue (still with the hedge on your left) over a third hill to an ancient barn in the far left hand corner of the field. Just beyond the barn, turn left through a gate and follow a green lane, first between two hedges and then alongside a hedge on the left.

Bend right along this lane and then left. The spire to the south east is that of Burton in Lonsdale Church. As with the lane on the way to Tunstall the verges of this little overgrown highway can be luxuriant at the right time of year. Continue over yet another hill and down into a small dip. Go through the gate in front and keep straight ahead. The hedge should now be on your right. After about 200 yards another track appears from the left. Keep straight ahead (right) along this new track to a gate. Go through this and pass two bungalows and the entrance to Laithbutts Farm on the right. You are now on a metalled road. Follow this for about a mile, and go under a railway bridge to the A65. There are splendid views of Gragareth ahead.

This hill might have been 'the range of snowy summits' which Charlotte mentions the girls would see on their way back from church in *Jane Eyre*. Assuming the girls did come this way, they would then have turned left along the old main road. No one in their right senses would do that now! So instead cross the main road to a wooden rail and steps on the far side and climb up to some steps and a stile. Over the stile follow the wall on the left until it bends left and then aim straight across to the corner of another wall ahead to the left of a large tree. Once here follow the hedge on the left to a stile in the corner of the field. Once over the stile, head for another stile in the middle of a short section of stone wall ahead. Cross this and head for a gate ahead, stopping to look up at the views of Gragareth to the east. All this land belongs to the Shuttleworth Estate.

Cross the stone bridge before the gate, then go through the gate and follow the clear trackway ahead to another gate in

The church at Leck, which Charlotte and Emily knew during their schooldays at Cowan Bridge School.

the corner of the field which leads into a metalled road. Turn left along the road and past Leck Church, where one or two of the girls from Cowan Bridge School are buried, until you come to a T-junction.

At the T-junction turn left. Then within 30 yards turn right through some metal gates into a field. Keep to the right of some sheds and then downhill. Do not go into the farmyard, but find a stile in the left hand corner and then walk down a short lane past another farmyard to a metalled road. Cross to a stile to the left of a concrete lamp-post and enter a small field. Ignore a gate to your right and take a stile just to the right of another gateway ahead. You are now just above Leck Beck.

Turn left along a good track. When this goes into a field, stay on the right hand side of the wire fence and walk between the fence and the beck. These may have been the beck and woodlands referred to in *Jane Eyre* as the place where the young Jane and Mary Ann Wilson used to wander. When the path widens out, head for the stile ahead. Cross it into a field and follow the right hand hedge round to another railway bridge. Go under this and through a gateway into a field. Bend half right to follow a wire fence to a stile in the right hand corner of the field. Climb over this. As you do so you will see Cowan Bridge School again a few yards away to the right across the main road.

Cross the road – with care! – to the stile opposite. Once through this you will find yourself on the old bridge again. Turn left and follow the pavement to the proximity of the BT telephone box and cross to the Methodist Church. Cross the road back again, turn right and then left at the corner past the shop. In a few yards you will see the Village Hall car park and your car.

3

'Shirley' Country, 'Briarmains' and 'Fieldhead'

Walking Distance: 8 miles

We begin from the Red House, Gomersal, the Briarmains of *Shirley*, where Charlotte stayed with her friends the Taylors, the Yorkes of the novel. After exploring the house, we make our way round to Brookroyd, where Ellen Nussey spent most of her life, and then walk into Birstall, a town whose streets Charlotte must often have frequented. After a brief visit to Birstall Church, which Charlotte would have attended and where Ellen is buried, we walk up to Oakwell Hall, the Fieldhead of *Shirley*. After a look round we then return through the grounds and fields to the Red House by a route almost certainly used by Charlotte and Mary Taylor. This last part of the route is to be the first leg of the newly extended Brontë Way.

Outside the heart of the large cities visited by the Brontës, no part of the Brontë country has altered more than the *Shirley* Country, the northern slopes, that is, of the Calder valley between Brughouse and Dewsbury. During the Brontës' time it was not much more heavily populated than the Worth Valley, which actually lost some population in the late 19th century. If there was a difference, it was not that there were more factories, it was that the *Shirley* Country had a gentler appearance, with more fields and woodlands.

The area first entered the lives of the Brontës with Mr Brontë's induction as a curate at Hartshead in 1811. During the following year, the area saw the Luddite troubles rise to a peak. The destruction of machinery on Hartshead Moor was followed in April by the attack on William Cartwright's Rawfolds Mill at Liversidge. This was followed in April by

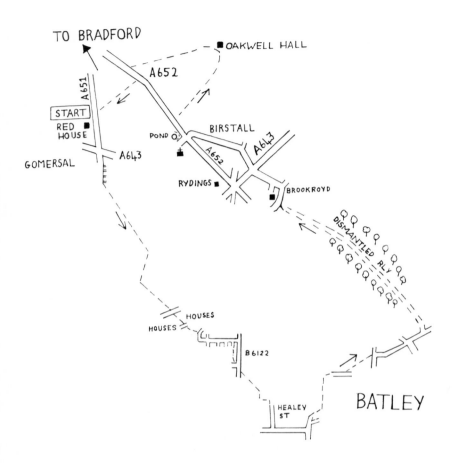

the murder of William Horsfall on Crossland Moor and the events consequent on that. All this Mr Brontë must have told over and over again to his young family. And these events were in due course to emerge in *Shirley*. But this was to be many years later.

Meantime Charlotte had got to know the area for herself. In 1831 she had been sent aged 14 to Miss Margaret Wooler's school at Roe Head on Dewsbury Moor. And there she had met in close succession her two lifelong friends, Mary Taylor and, a little later, Ellen Nussey. The school could not have been more different from Cowan Bridge. Much smaller, it attracted the daughters of the better off families around and taught them the ladylike accomplishments essential to their success in company. Given Mr Brontë's resources and commitments, it may seem surprising that Charlotte found her way there. In fact she would not have done if her godparents the Rev and Mrs Atkinson had not paid her fees for her. Mary Taylor was to remember her arrival at the school many years later:

'I first saw her coming out of a covered cart, in very old-fashioned clothes, and looking very old and miserable ... When she appeared in the schoolroom, her dress was changed, but just as old. She looked like a little old woman, so short-sighted that she always appeared to be seeking something, and moving her head from side to side to catch sight of it. She was very shy and nervous, and spoke with a strong Irish accent.'

Only a week or two later, Ellen Nussey, a distant relative of Mary Taylor, was also to arrive and Charlotte was no more enthusiastic about her. But after this cool start the three were to become firm friends who would increasingly visit each other's houses and meet together. Perhaps unexpectedly, in view of the later importance of Ellen, Mary Taylor was the first to break the ice. As she lived close to the school and often went home, she invited Charlotte to the Red House. With the astonishing photographic memory typical of her, Charlotte was to record for us in *Shirley* her first impressions:

'But if Briarmains chapel seemed alive, so also did Briarmains; though certainly the mansion appeared to enjoy a quieter phase of existence than the temple, some of whose windows too were aglow: the lower casements opened upon the lawn, curtains concealed the interior, and partly obscured the ray of the candles which lit it, but they did not entirely muffle the sound of voice and laughter. We are privileged to enter that front-door, and to penetrate to the domestic sanctum ... This is the usual sitting room of an evening. Those windows would be seen by daylight to be of brilliantly-stained glass – purple and amber the predominant hues, glittering round a gravely tinted medallion in the centre of each, representing the suave head of William Shakespeare, and the serene one of John Milton'.

So much for the house. How about its occupants? Even if we ignore their background, the Taylors were everything Charlotte was not – brash, confident, articulate, frank, democratic, republican and nonconformist – and, in Mary's case, a feminist to boot. Joshua Taylor, with all the confidence of a man whose family had counted for two centuries, combined fluency in several European languages with a determination to speak broad Yorkshire at home. Charlotte must inevitably have been shocked by much that she heard. However she did also have things in common with the Taylors. Mr Taylor was an avid reader in the literatures of the languages he spoke and he was generously to lend Charlotte many of the books she read to improve her French. She was to write later: 'The society of the Taylors is one of the most rousing pleasures I have known.' And her sheer enjoyment was, of course, to come out in her picture of the Yorkes and of Briarmains in *Shirley*, a picture whose accuracy is vouched for by Mary herself.

Surprisingly it was rather later that she was to visit Ellen's house, then still Rydings. It was to be in the autumn of 1834, when both had left school. Charlotte had come over with Branwell in a 2-wheeled gig and Ellen was to remember the impression the house and its grounds made on him: 'He walked about in unrestrained boyish enjoyment, taking views in every direction of the old turret-roofed house, the fine chestnut trees on the lawn . . . and a large rookery – all these he noted and commented upon with perfect enthusiasm. He told his sister he was leaving her in Paradise.' And she was also to give us a revealing thumbnail sketch of Charlotte's reactions, too, commenting upon her sensitivity and her 'estrangement' (Ellen's own word) at being away from home. She recalled how much time her friend spent away from the house, wandering through the plantations and in the fruit

The Red House, family home of Mary Taylor, lifelong friend of Charlotte Brontë. It was portrayed as 'Briarmains' in Shirley.

garden. It was a side of Charlotte that has not always been noticed – and one that she never lost.

It was as well that Charlotte had so steeped herself in this atmosphere. There was only to be one more visit – in late February and March 1835, when Ellen asked Charlotte over for a month and Charlotte stayed a fortnight. As early as 1834 the forthcoming marriage of Richard Nussey and the death of Ellen's aunt at Brookroyd nearby had portended change. By the end of 1836, Richard had moved with his new wife, and some of his new family, into Rydings and Ellen had moved with her mother and brothers and sisters into Brookroyd. No doubt Charlotte would still have visited Rydings from time to time; but from now on it was to be at Brookroyd that she – increasingly frequently – stayed.

During the late 1830s and much of the decade that followed, the Spen Valley became the very hub of Charlotte's life outside the Parsonage. The close three-sided friendship expanded to take in other members of the Taylor family as well as Ellen's brothers and sisters.

However, the idyll had to end. By the early 1840s, the reduced circumstances of her family, the death of her father and her own radical feminism had convinced Mary of the views that she later voiced in her book, *The First Duty of Women* – that women ought to be able to stand on their own feet. As part and parcel of this she urged Charlotte and Emily to go to Brussels to complete their education. And a little later she too followed them and joined her sister Martha there. After so long an interval the old school friends were re-united again. But this oddly was to be the parting of the ways. After Martha's sudden death Mary set about making a career for herself in real earnest. Firstly she went to Germany, where she learnt German whilst teaching some young boys English. Increasingly, however, her thoughts were turning to an idea first mooted between herself and her dead sister – of making a new life for herself in New Zealand. So after a brief holiday in England and then a short visit to bid goodbye to her old friends she set sail in February 1845 for the other side of the world. Charlotte was never to see her again.

Such was the nature of the two personalities that Ellen could not fill the gap left by Mary. Nonetheless Ellen became increasingly not just a valued confidante in all the troubles that lay ahead, but almost a surrogate sister. And the part played by Ellen in those last years is a moving testimony to the value of a deep and genuine friendship.

But friendships were not quite all that the Spen Valley area provided for Charlotte. As she launched into her serious fiction Charlotte was to draw repeatedly upon the people and places of the area for inspiration. In *The Professor*, Joshua Taylor was to re-appear as Hunsden Yorke Hunsden (Hunsden is a reminiscence of Hunsworth where the Taylors owned a mill). In *Jane Eyre* Charlotte used her memories of Rydings and its grounds to create her Thornfield Hall. (The mid Calder valley was contributing far more to her literary landscapes than Haworth itself was.) Indeed in *Shirley*, the country and its people were to oust almost everything else. It was as if after the traumatising events of the last two years, leaving her alone in the world – with Branwell, Emily and Anne all gone – she could only come to terms with herself by living over again the events of her now departing youth. Ostensibly set in the 1810s, the novel was really a depiction of the 1830s. All that Charlotte had lost she breathed into life again. The Taylors (Yorkes) were resident at the Red House again; all the family were alive and still as busily arguing as they had all those years earlier; Joshua Taylor presided, benignly radical, over them all. Into this sunlit world she introduced her father, the Rev Helstone, a young vigorous man again and her brilliant and wayward sister, Shirley Keeldar. All personal pain is exorcised in an ending that is all the more poignant by our awareness of its impossibility. Nowhere else perhaps as one walks in the footsteps of Charlotte and her friends is one so aware not just of the fiction, but the dreams and the regrets that preceded it all.

THE WALK FROM GOMERSAL TO OAKWELL HALL, VIA BIRSTALL

Park in the car park of the Red House Museum at Gomersal on the A651, Bradford to Heckmondwike Road. This is where Charlotte's friend, Mary Taylor, and her family lived. Charlotte visited and stayed at the house several times and made it the model for Briarmains in *Shirley*, as Mary herself conceded. After having a good look round the house, leave by the car park, cross the road and turn right (south). When you reach the A643 cross the A651 and walk down Spen Lane until you are opposite the church, Gomersal Parish Church. This is where Mary Taylor is buried. The grave can be found by keeping the church to your left when you enter the churchyard and walking to the end (the west end). Mary Taylor's grave will be found 30 yards beyond the tower – almost at the end of the graveyard. There can be a fine view from the spot into the Pennines.

After having visited the grave, retrace your steps back to the road and the crossroads. Cross the A651 and turn right.

Once you are on the south side of the A643, Church Lane, walk past the end of five streets on your left. Immediately past the shop (Gomersal Grocers) turn left along a cinder track. Pass through several gates. When you reach a T-junction of footpaths keep straight ahead into the field in front of you following the fence on your right. At the next gateway and stile follow the clear path half right down the field to a hedge corner. Just past this you will find a stile almost in the corner on your left. Cross this stile and then aim half right along a clear path towards the main road ahead.

When you reach the road cross over to a footpath which goes between the houses on the far side. At the end of this path cross another – much quieter – road to another path between the houses on the far side. Follow this and when you reach a third road, Leeds Old Road, turn left for 20–30 yards to cross to yet another path through housing. At the end of this you will find yourself in Lawrence Crescent. Turn right and follow the crescent round to another road. Here turn right for a few yards, then turn left into Lee Side Road. Walk ahead along this. Pass two roads off to the right. When you reach a third one, White Lee Side, turn right along it. In turn this changes from a road to a footpath between the houses and then into a rough lane. Follow it through to the end and then turn left into Dale Lane. At the end of Dale Lane turn right into the busy White Lee Road.

Keep along the right hand pavement until you see a footpath sign and stile on the opposite side of the road. This is at the end of a length of crenellated stone wall. Cross over the road to this and once over the stile aim half right along the clear path towards the left hand side of a small thicket of hawthorn trees below one or two new houses. From here follow the path, keeping close to the trees to a stile in the corner below the new houses. Go through the stile and follow the footpath round and right into a sandy lane. Now keep left and above the new houses and then follow the path as it begins to veer right and uphill alongside a wall above a field. (It sounds more complicated than it is!) When you reach a close, walk a few yards ahead along the close and then take the footpath to the left of Ashley Lee. At the end of this path you will emerge into Healey Street. Walk down this street to the end and then turn left along Healey Lane. There are some pleasant old-fashioned shops along the left hand side of the street.

Keep straight along Healey Lane until the road turns right, keeping The George Inn on your right. About 200 yards further fork left along Towngate Road, then turn left into Chaster Street. Cross the stile ahead and then follow the broad track as it curves first right and then left along the top and then the right hand side of the field. When you are nearly at the bottom of the field, turn right through a stile and pass along the right hand side of some recreation grounds. Walk into the unmade North Bank Road. When North Bank Road turns right – and gets a good surface – turn half left on to the recreation ground and walk downhill towards the road ahead aiming towards a brick mill chimney. When you are near the main road aim for the Lord Nelson inn.

Cross the road, turn right and then left along Centenary Way. Walk to the end, turn left and then almost immediately right up Carlinghow Hill. Immediately after the demolished railway bridge turn left below the impressive Victorian complex into Transvaal Terrace. Where this curves right, keep along the stone wall to your left and you will come to a stile. This takes you on to the Linear Walk along the trackbed of the old railway line. Turn right along this and walk along the trackbed for about ⅔ mile. Do not leave the track bed. In succession you will pass through woods and a public park, Wilton Park. As the path along the trackbed comes to an end follow a path into the park. Walk towards the road ahead, Brookroyd Lane. As you approach the road, leave the park by the higher, the right hand one, of the two gateways.

Turn right past Oak View Terrace and curve left with the road itself until you see Brookroyd Gardens on the left. Turn left down this street for a few yards. The impressive, plain fronted Victorian villa called Brookroyd visible through the hedge is the house in which Ellen Nussey lived after the family left Rydings in 1837. Charlotte visited the house several times. Indeed it was there that she corrected the proofs of *Jane Eyre* in September 1847. After looking at Brookroyd return to Brookroyd Lane and turn left. It is probably safest to cross over and follow the right hand pavement. Walk to the end of Brookroyd Lane and the busy Huddersfield Road.

Here the walker must make a decision. Rydings, the more impressive house, in which Ellen was living when Charlotte first visited her in September 1832, is situated about ¼ mile away down to the left beyond the very busy road junction. It is anything but a scenic journey, it has to be said. Rydings is on private land, surrounded by industrial premises and not very much of it is visible. If you would like to see the house, keep along the pavement on the left hand side of the road and walk down to the crossroads. Cross with exceptional care – traffic can come from any two of six different directions – and keeping to the left hand pavement walk uphill until you are opposite the Leyland Paint Buildings. If you station yourself on the opposite side of the road to the access road between the buildings you will see a stone wall with a gateway in it. The ancient-looking crenellated building to the right of this gateway is Rydings, almost certainly one of the models for Thornfield Hall in *Jane Eyre*. After taking a distant look at the house return on the same side of the road to the end of Brookroyd Lane.

From the end of Brookroyd Lane cross the busy Huddersfield Road to the street opposite, Chapel Street. Walk uphill to the centre of Birstall. If you turn left you are now on Low Lane. Keep on the left hand pavement as it snakes its way through the small town, following it round left when it changes its name first to Cross Street and then Kirkgate. Cross Bradford Road and follow the rest of Kirkgate to Birstall Parish Church (almost certainly closed). This is the church at which the Nusseys worshipped. It seems almost certain that Charlotte also must have attended services here.

Only the square Norman tower survives from the period of the Brontës. The rest was rebuilt in 1863–70 (architect W. H. Crossland). However, the grave of the Nusseys – including Ellen's – can still be seen in the well-mown churchyard, as can the grave of Miss Wooler, Charlotte's old headmistress and friend.

After you have inspected the churchyard, cross over Kirkgate to the pond on the other side. Turn right and walk along the edge of the pond for approximately 75 yards. Then turn right at a footpath sign and walk down to and cross a wooden bridge to gain the main road. Turn left here in the direction indicated by another footpath sign and walk along the left hand pavement. Just before Monk Ings on the left, cross over the main road and follow signs pointing to Oakwell Hall. A good steady climb along a gravel drive will bring you to Oakwell Hall Country Park. Walk up the drive to the hall itself and have a good look round the 'Fieldhead' of *Shirley*. When you come out at the back, walk right round the

Oakwell Hall, 'Fieldhead' in Shirley. *This is where Charlotte imagined her sister Emily as resident, under the name Shirley Keeldar. The affinity with the now vanished High Sunderland Hall is striking.*

hall through the herb garden and then walk in front of the hall. Turn left and walk through the stile. Once through the stile turn immediately right to follow the clear gravel path. Go down some steps to a bridge across a beck and then follow the main track as it heads roughly in the direction of a mill chimney ahead. Pass the Countryside Centre and then walk through car parks along a sandy lane to the main road.

When you reach the main road (Bradford Road) turn left. Walk for a few yards until you reach a 40 mph sign. Here cross over and follow the sandy lane on the opposite side uphill. As you walk up this path which was almost certainly taken by Charlotte and her friends you will come as close to the quiet unspoiled nature of the old Spen Valley as is possible at this time. As you approach some buildings keep straight ahead, aiming for the left hand side of the buildings. You pass between a stone wall and a hedge and then two stone walls. At the end of this enclosed path turn right along a short track to the busy main road ahead.

The single storey uninspiring building just to the right, which is currently used as a garage, was built as a chapel by John Taylor. Now concrete faced, it was red brick when first built to house the radical Killhamite New Connection Methodists, who demanded more say for the layman. It is just possible this is the tabernacle satirised in Chapter 9 of *Shirley* (though it was not raw or new looking in the time of the Brontës and was certainly not Wesleyan).

Turn left along the main road. After 100 yards you will see the Red House Museum car park on your right across the road.

4

Keighley: The Brontës' Gateway To The World

Walking Distance: 9 miles (or 5 miles)

The walk falls into two parts. During the first part we follow the newly established Worth Way up and down the hills to the east of the Worth Valley along a route which gives us some idea of the way the Worth Valley looked in the time of the Brontës, a mixture of fields and small hamlets, heathery hillsides and wooded valley-bottoms. En route we call in at the pub where Branwell's Halifax friends always claimed they had heard him read some of *Wuthering Heights*. When we reach Haworth we turn round and follow the other side of the valley back into Keighley. This was the route used by many Haworth residents well into the present century and it is as good as certain that this was the route walked by the Brontës themselves. Should time or inclination not allow for the whole walk, there is a 20 minute bus service and a train service from Haworth back to Keighley, shortening the walk to 5 miles.

Keighley has never been at the centre of Brontë pilgrimages. It does not seem to figure in any of the Brontë writings. And on its side Keighley has never put itself out to attract lovers of the Brontës. One suspects if Keighley people did think about the Brontës at all after their deaths it would have been in the manner described by Sir Wemyss Reid, an early biographer. 'What was peculiar to Yorkshire' he remembered in his own life, 'was the fact that, if you mentioned the name of Brontë in any average company, the chances were in favour of your being met with an indignant snort from

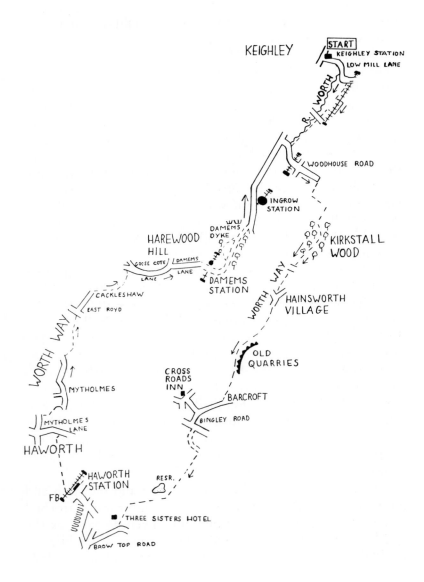

someone who protested that Charlotte's stories were a disgraceful libel upon the district, and that *Wuthering Heights* was a book so dreadful that its author would only have met with her just deserts if she had been soundly whipped for writing it.'

However, at all stages during the family's lives the town played its own crucial if largely hidden part. So what sort of place was it? Like many industrial towns of the old West Riding, it was a bit of a newcomer. Little more than a village originally, its fortunes had been transformed by the building of the Leeds–Liverpool canal and then, in 1847, by the arrival of the railway. Whitaker, the historian of Craven put it succinctly: 'Before the introduction of manufactories, the parish of Keighley did not want its retired glens and well-wooded hills; but the clear mountain torrent now is defiled, its scaly inhabitants suffocated by filth, its murmurs lost in the din of machinery . . .'

This is no less than the truth, in the first half of the 19th century, Keighley was a boom-town. In the course of their lives the Brontës would have seen no fewer than 30 mills spring up, many actually along the banks of the becks flowing down into the Aire. However, bits of the past survived. The occasional thatched cottage still lingered in the centre. The main shopping street still had something of the air of a Victorian Christmas card. The low shops had tiny-paned bow-windows. The town huddled around its parish church as it had done for centuries. And though many of the buildings are different now, something of the atmosphere of the old Keighley can still be seen in the corner round the parish church.

It was a town then of contrasts – new and old, rich and poor, squalid and picturesque, polluted and rural, parochial and yet a little local metropolis, too. Even as early as the 1820s, it far outclassed Haworth in its range of facilities. It could boast hairdressers, a savings bank, oil and colour dealers, several bookshops and stationers, watch and clock makers, a technical and at least two circulating libraries, an

insurance office, a range of milliners and drapers, foodshops
of every kind, a market of its own. And commonsense alone
would suggest that all the Brontës – Aunt Branwell included
– must have repeatedly made their way down into Keighley
and out again. That is where they had to go if they wanted
anything out of the ordinary or to travel any distance. That is
where they banked, Aunt Branwell at the local branch of the
Craven Bank, Mr Brontë at the Keighley Savings Bank. And it
was to Keighley that they would have gone to take a coach or
catch a train to all those increasingly far flung places they
began to visit later in life.

But Keighley was much more important than this. The
Brontës had several sets of friends in Keighley. The most
significant of these was Mr Brontë's friend, the Rev Theodore
Dury, the Rector of Keighley. Mr Dury may have put Mr
Brontë on to Cowan Bridge School, to which he had sent his
own daughter. By 1828 Mr Brontë had joined Mr Dury and
other local worthies on the Board of Trustees of the Keighley
Savings Bank. (He was to remain one until 1857). In 1832–
33, some seven or eight years after its foundation, Mr Brontë
joined the Keighley Mechanics Institute, where he would
have been bound to encounter Mr Dury. Aunt Branwell
seems to have got on with the Dury family sufficiently well to
choose Mr Dury as one of the executors of her will when she
drew that up on 30 April 1833. This friendship may have
influenced events in Charlotte's life on one occasion. It has
long been a puzzle as to how it came about that Charlotte
went to work at Stone Gappe in Lothersdale. Her usual
contacts, the Miss Woolers, were almost certainly not
involved. However, there were two people in an excellent
position to arrange it – the Rev Theodore Dury and his wife.
The Reverend Dury was the brother-in-law of Mrs Sidgwick
of Stone Gappe. Who better placed than him, then, to know
that Mrs Sidgwick was in the last stages of pregnancy, had
lost her previous governess and was urgently seeking a re-
placement? If this is so, it makes Charlotte's grumble about
Mrs Sidgwick's not knowing her and not even intending to

Keighley parish church gates. This is perhaps as close as we can now come to the Keighley of the Brontës.

get to know her rather less extraordinary than it might seem. If she had been introduced by a long-standing friend of her father's she might well feel she had legitimate cause for complaint!

However the main part which Keighley played in the lives of the family was as a source of reading matter. The Brontës' favourite newspapers, the *Leeds Intelligencer* and the *Leeds Mercury* could only be obtained in Keighley and Charlotte's earliest autobiographical fragment alludes to 'papa and Branwell' as having 'gone to Keighly . . . for the paper, the *Leeds Intelligencer*, a most excellent Tory newspaper'. And it was to Keighley that they also went for their books. For the last 40 or so years it has been generally assumed that they got these from the Library of the Keighley Mechanics Institute, but there is no record of Mr Brontë having joined the Institute until 1832–33. So the young Brontës could not have borrowed books there before that date. Borrowing books was a privilege confined to members.

Moreover it is not very likely that they borrowed much

after this. Both the stock and the Rules of the Library are still to be found in Keighley Library. And the Rules show that the Library was only open for borrowing for one hour on a Monday and a Friday evening. Only one son at a time could accompany the father to the Library and only one book could be borrowed at a time. There is no mention at all of daughters. So if the girls did walk down to Keighley to get their books – and there is good evidence for this – where did they go? The answer is that they borrowed from the usual source used by the Victorians, a circulating library, which would usually be run as part of another business. There may have been none of these in Haworth, as a letter to Ellen Nussey shows, but we know of at least two in Keighley, both of which may have been patronised by the Brontës. There was a circulating library on the premises of Robert Aked who printed two treatises by Mr Brontë. There was another one on the premises of a Mr Hudson who appears in the town directories of the time as a bookseller. And interestingly some personal reminiscences of the Brontës by an old Haworth resident which appeared in the *Bradford Observer* on 17 February 1894 speaks of Charlotte's specifically using Mr Hudson's library, whilst another source, Gordon Bottomley, the Keighley-born poet, mentions in a memoir of his father, that the Brontë girls used to call in and have a chat with the wife of the local doctor, Dr John Milligan, an old Haworth girl, when they walked into and out of Keighley to change their library books 'at a Keighley circulating library'.

This may seem rather academic. In fact it is anything but. It tells us that the Brontë girls were rather different in their reading tastes from what has been supposed – that they were much closer, in fact, in their tastes to most 'late Hanoverian' young ladies. What they were interested in was not the earnest scientific tomes that formed so much of the staple of the Keighley Mechanics Institute but the lighter reading to be obtained at circulating libraries. We ought not to go too far in this, of course. Although the stock-lists of the Keighley libraries do not seem to survive, records of the ones from

Calderdale that do, suggest that good solid reading too formed a part of the average stock, but there was also plenty of humour and 'romance' in the modern sense, not to mention potboilers and Gothic novels. The girls' trips into Keighley then, would have been a bit of light relief within their hard-working lives, during which they might hope to get the latest 'best-seller' and catch up on the latest gossip over tea with friends.

THE WALK FROM KEIGHLEY TO HAWORTH AND BACK

Apart from short walks round Haworth itself, the walk which the Brontës would have done most was the one from Haworth to Keighley and back. As this book centres on walks which they actually did or wrote about, this creates some problems. Although there is some attractive scenery all the way between the two communities, there is also much urban development. To cater for different tastes then, this walk is presented in bipartite form. Section A (Keighley to Haworth, 5 miles) is an attractive up and down route following the newly established Worth Way which shows what the Worth Valley would have been like in the time of the Brontës and calls in on one of Branwell's haunts, the Cross Roads Inn, before winding its way up into Haworth. Section B (Haworth to Keighley, 4 miles) is substantially the route taken by the Brontës themselves – and many other Haworth residents. What it gains over the other leg of the walk in authenticity however, it loses in attractiveness and towards the end involves over half a mile of main road walking. For those intimidated by this prospect it might be better to catch the train back to Keighley from either Damems station or Ingrow, a fascinating complex in its own right, or, if that is inconvenient, to take the bus. Buses run at 20 minute intervals.

Section A

This section of the walk begins from Keighley railway station, from which the new Worth Way begins and from which the Brontës made so many journeys to and from home after the opening of the station on 16 March 1847. The layout of the station and area was very different from now. The road then crossed the line by a level crossing and the station was on the opposite side of the road.

Starting, however, from the present station, turn left as you come out of the buildings and left again down Low Mill Lane until you cross the river Worth. Pass by the entrance to the Yorkshire Electricity premises and then turn right along a ginnel with a sign indicating the Worth Way. After 200 yards go through a short 'foot-tunnel' and climb uphill. At the footbridge on your right, turn right over the old Keighley to Queensbury line. Over the bridge, follow the path to the left and then to the right through another foot-tunnel, this time under the Keighley and Worth Valley Light Railway (KWVLR). Now turn left and cross over Park Lane to a metalled road with a 'No Through Road' sign. You should see a Worth Way sign pointing the way. After about 50 yards fork left uphill on an unpaved path between the railway and some industrial buildings. Continue ahead when you meet the river Worth. This part of the way is astonishingly quiet and secluded considering that you are in the heart of Keighley. Follow the river-bank until you come to 12 stone steps. Climb up these and turn left into Woodhouse Road.

Now walk uphill crossing the bridge over the KWVLR and then Hainsworth Road and Woodhouse Drive. When the road abruptly ends turn right on the signed public footpath (also posted with a Worth Way sign) and climb steeply uphill. As you climb extensive views will open up across Keighley and the upper Worth Valley. On reaching the top of the path, go through a kissing gate and over a stone stile to the left in the wall and turn right along a gravel path. Walk up this for between 100 and 200 yards, then turn right into a wood along a path posted with the usual Public Footpath and

Worth Way signs. The path through this surprisingly rocky woodland should be easy enough to follow, but if in doubt, keep a short distance to the left of the wall on the right. At the end of the wood go through a gap stile and walk half left across the field to where there are two gateways side by side. Go through the left hand gate. Keeping the wall on your right now go through four fields in succession by way of stiles. At the end of the fourth field turn right through a stile in the wall on your right at the far end of the field. Now turn left through a paddock and walk ahead to a gate-stile to the left of a gate. Through this continue along a rough lane to a metalled road. Cross over the road and walk straight ahead on the gravel track. You are now in the hamlet of Hainsworth.

Follow this track for 300 yards and when it forks take the left-hand fork uphill. It is again posted with a Worth Way sign. When a small path deviates left into a quarry continue on the main path as it makes its way first between the quarries and houses and then between the quarries and fields. In August and early September this path can be amongst the most colourful in the whole of the Brontë Country. After about ¾ mile of this enchanting path turn right on to a metalled road, Bingley Road, and walk downhill through the hamlet of Barcroft. When Bingley Road divides in two – both called Bingley Road! – opposite to Lane End, turn right and walk down the right hand branch of Bingley Road to the main road. On the opposite side you will see the Cross Roads Inn, which serves real ale and bar snacks. This is genuinely one of the pubs frequented by Branwell – perhaps because it was not quite so under the eye of the Parsonage! And it was here – misprinted as the Cross Hands Inn – that William Dearden and other Halifax friends claimed to have heard Branwell read out *Wuthering Heights* to his assembled friends.

Whether you choose merely to gaze across at this literary shrine or to follow in the footsteps of Branwell, turn back up Bingley Road and return to the top opposite to Lane End. This time turn right along the other branch of Bingley Road

The Cross Roads Inn, where Branwell read extracts from Wuthering Heights, *according to his Halifax friends.*

and walk down to the busy A629 again. Bear right for a few yards then turn very sharp left down a lane on the far side of the road (taking extra care if you have been following Branwell's example too enthusiastically). You follow this through a sort of Z-bend, then when you reach some houses to the left turn right through a stile by a gate. At this point you are leaving the Worth Way.

Once through the stile, walk alongside the wall on the right towards a small lake (dam) ahead. As you come level with the lake, climb half left uphill, but when you pass through a ruined wall do not continue to climb but contour round the hill on the clear path ahead. This eventually meets a wall on the right. When it does so follow the wall until you emerge on to a tarmac driveway. Follow this drive above the Three Sisters up to the road. Here keeping to the right hand side of the road turn downhill. After about 200 yards you will meet a pavement. Follow this down to the main road, Hebden Road, and cross into Brow Road. Walk down the steps and pavement on the right hand side. When the road bends to the left walk ahead along Victoria Road. This is the most authentic, least 'touristy' part of Haworth. When you come to Apsley Street turn left and walk down the street and then the path between the houses. When you come out into Mill Hey at the bottom turn left and cross. From here you can get the bus or train back to Keighley.

If on the other hand you wish to complete the walk by climbing up to the centre of Haworth turn left in front of the station and just past the station go over the railway by the wooden footbridge. At the far side of the bridge turn sharp right up an old lane that slopes uphill to the left of and above a house and garden. When after a few yards the path divides keep straight ahead towards a group of cottages and farm buildings. Turn left in front of these and walk along them. Then immediately past the garage at the end, turn right and walk ahead to a gate and stile. Once through this take the left fork along the path by the wall. At the top of this go through a stile and turn right along a ginnel. At the end of the ginnel turn left into Mytholmes Lane and walk uphill. When you reach the top of Mytholmes Lane look out for Changegate ahead. Walk up to this and turn left. You are now in the historic heart of Haworth and a few yards walk further will bring you to the top of the Main Street and the church.

Section B

With you back to the church steps cross the Main Street and turn left down Changegate, on the far side of the Tourist Information Centre. Walk ahead at the crossroads. When opposite a large stone house on the left, turn right down a road marked Private Access and walk to the left of a new building along a path between a wall and a fence. When you emerge into some land at the back of a long row of houses continue ahead until you reach a gate on your left. The correct footpath goes down a stone ramp into a hen-run and then out of the hen-run by a gate to the right of a henhouse. Through this gate walk down to an enclosed path which runs downhill to the left of a small housing estate. When you reach the end of the garden on your right, shortly before two stone pillars, cross a stile on your right into a field. With your back to this, walk half left to a stile leading into a thicket. There is to be some housing development here. At the present time follow the clear path downhill through the trees to the bare ground below and turn right into Baden Street.

At the end of Baden Street turn left down Victoria Avenue through the community of Mytholmes. Cross the river Worth and walk uphill past Hebble Row on your left. Opposite a pair of stone Victorian houses turn right up some steps posted Public Footpath and Worth Way. (For those doing the whole walk you have omitted about four miles and now rejoined it on its way back to Keighley.) Follow the path between stone walls, fences, etc. Do not deviate from the path until the main route swings left and there is a metal kissing gate in front of you. Go through this kissing gate into a field and follow the clear path half left to a gate and a kissing gate. On the main road, turn left as directed by the Worth Way sign and then turn right along East Road. (Ignore the Private Road signs: this is a public footpath.) Where a footpath branches left, keep straight ahead along the private road to New House Farm and 18 New House. Walk through the farmyard and out at the far end, by a stile; immediately through the stile, turn right before a stone garage and follow the walled path between two farms to a gate with a stile to its left. Go through the stile and walk ahead with a wall on your right across most of two fields, but before the end of the second field veer a little to the left to a stile in the wall ahead. Once through the stile climb the next field to a gap in the wall. Go through this and head for a step-stile by another stone garage. Over the stile turn left to the road, Goose Cote Lane. Cross to the far pavement.

Turn right downhill along this road, go round a corner and then turn right down Damems Lane. There should be a Worth Way sign. When the metalled surface ends continue along the stone track past Damems Station with its fine

A stretch of the Worth Way, between Keighley and Haworth, not very far from the Cross Roads Inn.

signal-box. If any of the party are flagging it is possible to take the train from here either to Keighley or Haworth. Otherwise cross the river Worth and turn left along the broad track. The Worth Way continues straight along this, but it is more interesting if you go through a stile on the left in about 300 yards and walk through the Damems Dyke Nature Reserve. The best route is to keep left and follow the river bank until you can go no further and then to curve back to the main track and turn left. In a few yards you will reach the main road.

Now begins the least attractive part of the walk. Follow the main road down to Ingrow Station, formerly Foulridge Railway Station. It is worth looking round here if you have time. The former goods yard also houses the headquarters of the Bahamas Locomotive Society. If you are exhausted by now or cannot face the roadwalk ahead, you can catch either the train or bus to Haworth or Keighley.

When you have had a look round, continue along the main road past a series of industrial premises until you reach

Woodhouse Road. Turn right. When you have crossed the bridge over the river Worth, descend the steps to the path along the right hand bank of the river. Follow this path until it veers off to the right of an industrial building. Walk straight ahead with the building to the left and the railway to the right. When you reach a road turn right along it to the busy road ahead. Cross this with care keeping the railway bridge to your right. On the far side turn immediately right through a footway under the railway and follow the flagged path first left and then right over a footbridge across a disused railway. Over this turn left to go down another flagged path and under another footway under the railway. The railway should now be on your right again. Continue ahead between a wall and railway until you reach a road. Turn left along this noting the setts, the typical road surface used in many areas in the time of the Brontës. Walk ahead across the river Worth to the main road. Keighley Station is a few yards away to the right.

5

Southowram, Law Hill and High Sunderland Hall

Walking Distance: 6 miles

We begin from Shibden Hall, the finest house in the Shibden valley and one sometimes identified with Thrushcross Grange. From here we walk up to Law Hill by the route which Emily would probably have used if she did walk between the school and the hall. From there we walk through the village of Bank Top as closely as we now can on the old route northwards from Southowram taking in Beacon Hill with its stunning view of Halifax. After walking through Claremount we visit the site of High Sunderland Hall, the original of Wuthering Heights house. We then return by Black Boy House, whose name may have suggested the ethnic origin of Heathcliff, and the once heavily quarried sides of the Shibden valley which Emily may also have had in mind when writing the novel.

Considering how close it is to Halifax, the Southowram area, under which I include much of the upper Shibden valley and the ridge between it and Halifax, has changed little since the time that Emily spent teaching at Miss Patchett's academy at Law Hill. New houses have been built, a housing estate or two has been tagged on to an existing community and some houses have been demolished. The area has also been criss-crossed by some trunk roads. By and large though what we see is what Emily would have seen – bracing green uplands, countless small fields, isolated farms, small dense woods and above all the deep, steep-sided ravine of the Shibden valley with, at its heart, Shibden Hall. To anyone who takes the trouble to walk this country there seems not the most minimal of reasons to associate the area with *Wuthering Heights*.

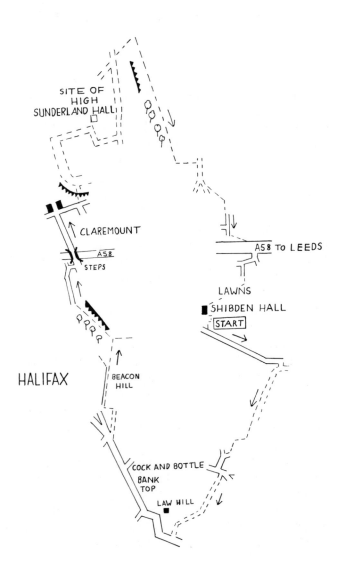

SITE OF
HIGH
SUNDERLAND HALL

CLAREMOUNT

A58

STEPS

A58 TO LEEDS

LAWNS

SHIBDEN HALL

START

HALIFAX

BEACON
HILL

COCK AND BOTTLE

BANK
TOP

LAW HILL

Yet we know now for a fact Emily did have some features of this area in mind.

At some point in the late 1830s Emily taught for a while at the Law Hill School. It seems likely that the cause of this was the marriage of one of the Miss Patchetts, Marie Patchett, to Titus Senior Brooke, a member of the extensive and wealthy Brooke family, some of whose members Charlotte had got to know at Roe Head. Charlotte may have got to know about this 'on the grapevine' and Emily volunteered or was pressurised into helping out family finances by taking up the position Miss Patchett had left vacant.

Miss Patchett and her sisters were part of an extensive and wealthy local family. Given the Patchetts' background, it is no surprise that Law Hill house, the second property which Miss Patchett had taken for her school, was an impressive building in an equally impressive situation. There were five large bedrooms on the first floor and five attics above them — a similar arrangement, though on a grander scale, to that in the house Wuthering Heights. And presumably, as in

Shibden Hall, thought by some to be the original model for 'Thrushcross Grange' in Wuthering Heights.

Wuthering Heights, the large bedrooms were reserved for the more important people, the garrets for the domestic staff.

So much for the house and school. But Law Hill was also a farm and the land behind it, still unbuilt on, was its farmland. For the only time in her life Emily would have found herself living on a working farm, where, as in *Wuthering Heights*, there were cattle to be milked, poultry to be fed, rabbits to be culled and all the other activities mentioned — mostly parenthetically — in the novel. No wonder there was a story in Southowram that Law Hill actually was Wuthering Heights. This cannot be true, but we are beginning to see that Emily took bits and pieces of her life at Southowram to create, as in a collage, her great novel.

In this milieu it would seem Emily worked for very long hours. Charlotte writes: 'I have had one letter from her since her departure; it gives an appalling account of her duties — hard labour from 6 in the morning until near 11 at night, with only one half-hour of exercise between. This is slavery. I fear she will never stand it.'

However in spite of her long hours, she did get some relaxation. As well as taking her pupils to and from the church at Southowram she also took other walks, including trips into Halifax to see the Museum. More importantly the verse fragments produced at this time show Emily was busily writing in such spare time as she had both *Gondal* and personal poetry. Some may give us fleeting insights into her feelings there:

> 'O come with me, thus ran the song
> The moon is bright in Autumn's sky
> And thou has toiled and laboured long
> With aching head and weary eye'

> 'And I entered the walls of my dark prison-house
> Mysterious it rose from the billowy moor.'

As I have said then, many local people saw Law Hill itself as the model for Wuthering Heights. And there is something

Law Hill, where Emily spent some time teaching in 1838 and which provided some of the inspiration and details for her novel Wuthering Heights.

to be said for this. It stands high on a hilltop exposed to the howling of the wind, the origin of the name. As Emily went about her teaching duties she would have seen the staff liming the fields, haymaking, leading the horses out to graze, all the activities so carefully alluded to in *Wuthering Heights*. Again the house is three storeys high, something Wuthering Heights is, too, we notice, if we read attentively. More strikingly still Emily would certainly have heard the story as to how the house came to be built there – by one Jack Sharp, who, like Heathcliff, had ousted the original son and heir of the family which had adopted him.

However, there was a much closer model for Wuthering Heights to be found locally. This was High Sunderland Hall, an extravaganza in stone, which the Sunderland family had built in about 1630 when it was at its wealthiest and proudest. By the time Emily wandered up to see it, it was owned by a William Priestley of Coley Hall. Like many wealthy men of the time – including Heathcliff as owner of Thrushcross Grange – he did not live there himself, but rented it out. At this point the house was divided up into several 'units'. By the 1841 census a family named Wood lived in the main part of the house; and a labourer and various weavers occupied the rest. If Emily did ever venture inside it could only have been into one or two portions of the hall. But in fact she probably did not. Inside, High Sunderland Hall was in certain crucial respects different from Wuthering Heights. And it seems the best guess that she filled the interior of the shell with details culled from elsewhere.

However the exterior of the house, as described by Lockwood at the beginning of the novel, is startlingly similar to High Sunderland Hall. 'The narrow windows,' we are told, 'are deeply set in the wall, and the corners defended with large jutting stones. Before crossing the threshold, I paused to admire a quantity of grotesque carving lavished over the front, and especially about the principal door; above which, among a wilderness of crumbling griffins and shameless little boys, I detect the date 1500 and the name Hareton Earnshaw.' Not surprisingly some details are wrong. There never was a date on High Sunderland Hall, nor any name. Instead there was a rather grand coat of arms. And two of the most striking features of High Sunderland Hall have been omitted – the impressive Baroque gateway to the west and the stained glass windows. That said, it is amazing what has been retained: the sculpture above the Baroque gateway has been transferred to the front facade and the two naked giants of the original have been changed into shameless little boys. Otherwise Wuthering Heights is little more than a slimmed down, simplified version of High Sunderland. And it is tempting to guess that she may have taken sketches of bits and pieces of the building that caught her attention and used these later. This might explain why the details are so accurate, their assemblage slightly wrong.

In any event, there would have been no Wuthering Heights without High Sunderland Hall. This has been known for some time. What is not is that there are other buildings in the area which may also have contributed to the novel. Half a mile north of High Sunderland is a building which also seems to have existed when Emily was in the area. This is Black Boy House. Although I have made enquiries I have not yet found out how the house got its strange name. Sometimes such names are inn names but this does not seem likely here. What cannot be gainsaid is that it is a curious coincidence that almost the next house to High Sunderland had this name and Emily is at such pains to alert us to the dark colour of her hero. For she does not merely call him a gypsy, but lascar too, someone of that mixed race of Indians and East Indians who were typically to be found in great ports. The choice of Liverpool for the place where the child was found was, it seems, no accident. We know that Miss Patchett possessed a copy of John Horner's *Buildings in the Town and Parish of Halifax*, a book which contained material on High Sunderland. What we have discovered suggests that this does not totally explain Emily's knowledge of High Sunderland and its surroundings. Inspired perhaps in the first place by the book, she wandered up to look in detail at the great stone pile just below the skyline and then explored beyond it. Here, encountering Black Boy Farm and remembering the story of Jack Sharp, she realised it might be possible to weave the threads together. And her talent as a writer wove those threads into one of the greatest love stories in the English language.

THE WALK TO BANK TOP AND HIGH SUNDERLAND HALL

Park at the upper car park at Shibden Hall. It is ONLY possible to get there by driving from the direction of Halifax town centre on the A58 towards Leeds and following Shibden Hall signs once you have crossed the Hebble Valley. Other signs take you to the lower car park. Only at the upper car park is it possible to change and look round the hall after the walk (or go to the small café for refreshments).

With your back to the front of the hall walk right to the end of the building, turn left and at the end of the lawn turn right up some steps. Turn left at the top of these and climb up to the terrace above the formal garden. In the corner you will see some large stones. Some of these come from High Sunderland Hall, the now demolished house which almost certainly was the model for Emily's Wuthering Heights. It is not much to show for what was once one of the finest 17th century houses in England.

Turn right along the terrace and at the end walk through the gateway, cross to the path curving up from the right below, turn left and walk out to the main road. Turn left along the road and walk downhill for about ½ mile. Go past a farm and then turn right into Shibden Hall Croft, a 1990s housing development. When you meet a T-junction turn right and walk past a house called High Gables on the right. On the left you will see a stone track. Follow this up behind the houses as it curves first left and then right. Do not go through the gate but walk uphill. If Emily Brontë really did visit Shibden Hall whilst she was at Law Hill this must have been the path she used.

If you stop after about 300 feet of climbing you will see where High Sunderland Hall would once have stood below the rounded green hill to the north. At the top of the narrow lane cross a broader gravel lane and walk along the narrow path between the wall and the barbed wire fence. At the end of this go through a stile into a field and follow the flagged path right towards a farm and its buildings. Just before the corner of the field go through the stile on the left and walk ahead to a gravel lane. Follow the lane past the front of the row of cottages and then turn right. At the T-junction with a metalled road turn left and follow to another road. Here turn left for about 10 yards and then turn right up a narrow track to the right of a large grass mound. Follow this lane for 400 yards to the main road. Cross this busy road with care and turn right along the pavement. The house 30 yards ahead of you on the right – and strictly private – is Law Hill where

High Sunderland Hall, demolished in 1950; the exterior was the original of Wuthering Heights House.

Emily taught for a time in the late 1830s. There would have been an outstanding view of High Sunderland Hall from here.

After looking at the outside of Law Hill continue along the main road as it curves slightly right ahead. Hardly any of the houses which line the route would have been here in Emily's time. When you reach the Cock and Bottle inn on the right, a brief diversion down the road to the right will give you the best view of Law Hill as it stands whitewashed on its green hilltop. Whether you take the diversion or not walk on past the Manor House Inn and where the road forks just past Trooper Lane on the left walk up Green Lane on the right. Follow this for about ¼ mile. When you come to a gate turn left on a narrow walled path and then right on open moorland. There is an electrifying view of Halifax spread below you to the left. If it is a warm windless day you may care to sit on the summit by the beacon and notice the main buildings of the town, the Piece Hall, the Parish Church and the unmissable headquarters of Britain's largest building society!

After you have taken in the view continue ahead by the
main path, that is the broadest and highest up. When you
reach a T-junction of paths turn left and then take the
furthest left out of three paths ahead. There is a gateway to
the right of it. The path, mostly paved, goes straight downhill
for a while and then abruptly bends right to form a rake
down through the attractive deciduous woodland. When you
reach the road cross with great care and follow the pavement
downhill to the right. When the road forks take the right
hand fork and follow the main road ahead past some industrial premises on the left. Just before the main road you will
see some steps across the road on the right. Climb up these to
the bridge over the main road and turn left.

Once over the A58 walk straight ahead up Claremount
Road. The right hand pavement is probably the best. Go past
a church on the left and Bell Street on the right. Just before
two sets of industrial premises on both sides of the road turn
right up a gravel lane. When you reach a point where
footpaths cross over from right to left, turn and climb the
broad steep path up to the top of the hill. At the top of the hill
turn left and follow the excellent path along the wall. Just
before descending to the road at Dirk Carr turn right uphill.
When the track comes to a corner and turns right you are
standing only a few yards away from High Sunderland Hall.
It stood a few yards ahead through the stile on the left.
Nettles, as so often, mark the place where this dramatically
beautiful house once stood.

After drinking in the atmosphere, turn right and then left
and follow the track to a T-junction ahead. Here turn left and
walk past the totally rebuilt Lower High Sunderland Hall and
a little later the intriguingly named Black Boy House. When
another track comes in from the left walk a few yards further
on and then look carefully for a rather overgrown dell which
follows the side of the wall downhill to the right. It is a bit
like jungle warfare – the kids will love it – but there is a path.

At the bottom cross a fence into the very steep field below. Here walk in the same direction as you have been before for about 100 yards. Then turn very sharp right slightly downhill along a just discernible path. Note: it is very important not to lose too much height. Follow the tenuous path as it meanders at roughly the same level for perhaps 300 yards. When you reach a point above a large white farm below and another stone-coloured farm to its right, look for a muddy but very clear path downhill. Taking care not to slip, follow this downhill.

At the bottom turn right and head towards the very clear line of terraced houses on the far side of the valley. Another vague path will lead you to a wooden stile. When you have crossed this you will see two paths ahead. Walk down to the lower one to the right of a very low stone wall. Follow this over a brook and then alongside another low stone wall to another brook. This is a good deal wetter than its predecessor and needs some care in crossing. It is possible to do it and not get too wet by striding from stone to stone at the left hand edge of the marshy area. Alternatively – if the fence along the brook has not been re-instated do not waste time crossing but walk downhill to the bottom of the field and cross the stile. If the fence has re-appeared, however, it will be necessary to negotiate this slough of despond and then turn left and follow the brook downhill on its right hand side to the stile.

Once over the stile turn right on a sandy lane. When the lane forks take the left branch. After 50 yards or so look out for a flagged path to the left between the track and the wall. For some yards it runs alongside the track almost as if it were its pavement. Cross to this and when the track swings away to the right continue to follow the flagged path to a stile and some stone steps which will take you down into a field. Follow the clear flagged path across two fields to a gate. Through the gate follow the flags alongside the wall to another gate and stile. Go through this into the gravel lane ahead. When the now metalled lane swings to the right, walk ahead on a clear path through the garden centre ahead.

At the end turn left and walk up the paved path to the main road. There is a footpath on the opposite side of the road which leads fairly directly into Shibden Park but traffic does not always allow one to risk crossing here. Personally I find it safer to turn left down the pavement for perhaps 30 yards and then cross over with exceptional care to the cobbled lane branching off downhill on the far side. Follow this down to the bottom and then take the second road off to the left, signed Godley Gardens. Walk ahead along this to the end of the houses and then walk through the gap in the wall into Shibden Park.

Cross the road and then walk straight ahead until you come to another path. Here turn half right and climb uphill towards Shibden Hall and the car. If you have time it makes a fitting climax to the walk to have a leisurely look round the hall and its folk museum and gardens.

6

Nidderdale and Swarcliffe Hall

Walking Distance: 6 miles

Much of the time that Charlotte worked for the Sidgwicks she was actually at Swarcliffe Hall, Birstwith, Nidderdale. We begin from the parish church which she would have had to attend on Sundays, Hampsthwaite Parish Church, explore the lower part of Nidderdale and then return by the Nidderdale Way, some of which she may have used as her path to and from church.

It was probably Mr Dury, the Rector of Keighley who brought about Charlotte's period as a governess to the Sidgwick family, first at Stone Gappe and then at Swarcliffe Hall in Nidderdale.

So how precisely did Charlotte become a governess? In May 1839 Mrs Sidgwick was 7 months pregnant and had, it seems, no one to look after her children. So it was that somehow or other Charlotte arrived to take up a position as a temporary governess. By now there were four Sidgwick children – Margaret aged 11, William 10, Mathilda 6 and John Benson 3. It was the two youngest who were to be Charlotte's charges. Although she had been teaching for some time by now, this was her first position as an actual governess. From the start it does not seem to have been a great success. She soon realised that whatever her connections – whether through Mr Dury or possibly Mr Carter at the newly completed Lothersdale Church – here she was very decidedly one of the 'staff'. In two letters to Ellen – one now lost – she complained that not only did Mrs Sidgwick not know her but that she had obviously no intention of doing so. The only compensation was Mr Sidgwick. Charlotte tells us:

'One of the pleasantest afternoons I have spent here –
indeed the only one at all pleasant – was when Mr Sidgwick
walked out with his children, and I had orders to follow a
little behind. As he strolled on through his fields with his
magnificent Newfoundland dog at his side, he looked very
like what a frank, wealthy, Conservative gentleman ought
to be. He spoke freely and unaffectedly to the people he
met, and though he indulged his children and allowed them
to tease himself too much, he would not suffer them
grossly to insult others.'

It is the last sentence that reveals what was amiss. Even at
Roe Head, Charlotte had been more stoical about her lot
than happy with it, but she was at least teaching young
teenage ladies there. Now she had become nursery school
teacher expected, she told Ellen, 'to wipe the children's
smutty noses or tie their shoes or fetch their pinafores or set
them a chair' – and no doubt worse even than that. Charlotte's resentment is visible in every added phrase in turn. But
then would one nowadays expect a sixth form teacher to turn
overnight into a nanny?

Charlotte spent two or three weeks at Stone Gappe with its
'pleasant woods, winding white paths and green lawns' and

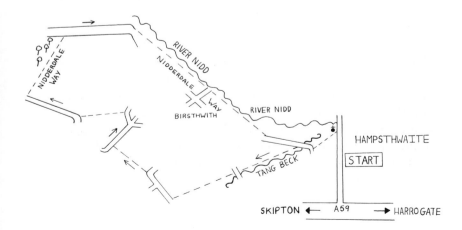

then at some point round 14 June the whole house adjourned to Swarcliffe Hall, high above the Nidd near Birstwith, to spend the early summer with Mrs Sidgwick's father. The Greenwoods had already pulled down the original building which stood on the site of the present Swarcliffe Hall, but the extensive rebuildings that brought it to its present size had still not taken place. Even so it was already an attractive house and in an even more beautiful position than Stone Gappe with its views across the woods and fields to the heather-topped heights across the dale. Disaffected as Charlotte was by now even she admitted it was a 'beautiful place in a beautiful country'. Sadly though she was to be even more unhappy here than in Airedale.

In part this was because she felt left out. The Sidgwicks and Greenwoods were an exceptionally sociable family and liked to turn family reunions into great social gatherings. Shooting parties were an important part of this. The house would often have been full of visitors then – family, local gentry, etc. Charlotte who was never good in large groups, even when she was lionised by people genuinely interested in her, would certainly have found it a strain.

'I would only ask you,' she wrote to Ellen Nussey, 'To imagine the miseries of a reserved wretch like me, thrown at once into the midst of a large family . . . at a time when they were particularly gay, when the house was full of company – all strangers, people whose faces I had never seen before.'

What made it worse was that with her lack of experience with very young children, she found it hard to cope with her charges – the 'pampered, spoilt and turbulent children', as she speaks of them to Ellen, whom she was expected 'constantly to amuse as well as instruct'. How bad they were we can only conjecture. However a story that rings true and is almost certainly based on a conversation between Charlotte and Mrs Gaskell appears in Chapter 8 of *The Life*. Although there are no names, it is clear that what we have here are the Sidgwick children.

'She had been entrusted with the care of a little boy, three

Swarcliffe Hall, where Charlotte was employed as a governess by the Sidgwick family.

or four years old, during the absence of his parents on a day's excursion, and particularly enjoined to keep him out of the stable-yard. His elder brother, a lad of eight or nine, and not a pupil of Miss Brontë's, tempted the little fellow into the forbidden place. She followed, and tried to induce him to come away; but, instigated by his brother, he began throwing stones at her, and one of them hit her so severe a blow on the temple that the lads were alarmed into obedience. The next day in full family conclave, the mother asked Miss Brontë what occasioned the mark on her forehead. She simply replied "An accident, ma'am," and no further inquiry was made; but the children (both brothers and sisters) had been present, and honoured her for not 'telling tales'. From that time she began to gain influence over all, more or less, according to their different characters; and as she insensibly gained their affection, her own interest in them was increasing. But one day, at the children's dinner, the small tyrant of the stable-yard, in a little demonstrative gush, said, putting his hand in hers, "I love 'ou, Miss Brontë". Whereupon the mother exclaimed before all the children, "Love the *gover-ness*, my dear!" A. C. Benson would only concede that his cousin had thrown a book at her, like the loathsome John Reid in *Jane Eyre*, and concluded acidly: 'It is clear that she had no gifts for the management of children.'

In any event, matters at Swarcliffe came to a head. 'At times,' Charlotte wrote to Ellen, 'I felt and I suppose seemed depressed. To my astonishment I was taken to task on the subject by Mrs Sidgwick with a stress of manner and a harshness of language scarcely credible. Like a fool I cried most bitterly; I could not help it.' And she continued that she had considered leaving for home at once; but she had reflected that it was not long to the summer holidays. Mrs Sidgwick began to behave 'more civilly', whilst even the children became 'a little more manageable'. So she stayed on until the family returned to Stone Gappe and about 19 July returned to Haworth full of plans for a holiday at the sea-side with Ellen.

The whole interlude must have seemed totally futile. In fact from a creative point of view it was the reverse. The two spoilt Sidgwick boys were to be amalgamated to form that unforgettable protrait of arrested male adolescence, the appalling John Reid, who could never do any harm in his doting mother's eyes; the girls became the insufferable In-grams reminiscing happily about the cruel tricks they had played on their long-suffering governesses. And E. F. Benson perceptively saw 'in the figures of the smart party, 'Baroness Ingram of Ingram Hall' and the rest, who swept about Mr Rochester's house' a ruthless caricature of the various guests who, with their 'callous gaiety', had so snubbed and ignored 'the silent little governess' at his cousins' house. Nor was this all she got out of her stay with the Sidgwicks, for it was almost certainly at Birstwith that she got her story of the madwoman in the attic, a legend attached to the nearby Norton Conyers. Herbert E. Wroot in his *Persons and Places* reported that 'Ellen Nussey remembered receiving from

Charlotte a verbal description of the place, and recalled the impression made on the mind of Charlotte by the story of the mad woman'.

THE WALK THROUGH NIDDERDALE

There are various places to park at Hampsthwaite which lies off the A59 Harrogate to Skipton road. There is often room along the village green; there is ample parking on the park of the village hall or it might well be possible just outside the church itself; failing all else there is a small patch of rough ground a few yards to the north of the bridge on the Hampsthwaite to Clint road.

In any event start at Hampsthwaite Church. Charlotte would have attended this church during the short period that she was at Swarcliffe Hall, but only the perpendicular west tower remains from the time when she was in Nidderdale. The 1820 church, which was itself new at the time, was replaced in 1902. If the church is open – which is not likely – it is possible to see pictures of the old church in the corner to the left of the south door. There is also a brass to Edwin Greenwood of Swarcliffe who was the owner of Swarcliffe Hall when Charlotte paid her visit in 1839.

Walk along the clear path to the left of the church. About 30 yards past the end of the tower, approximately 20 yards to the left of the path – near to the boundary fence of the part of the churchyard fenced off for sheep to graze – you can see the gravestone of Edwin Greenwood. If you have turned off to see this, return to the path and carry on ahead through a gate into a narrow shady trackway. When this joins a metalled road by a seat turn right. Walk 250 yards ahead to a stone bridge across a small stream, Tang Beck. Having crossed the bridge, turn left through a stile into a field. Follow the just visible path half right to walk roughly parallel to the hedge and the stream to the left.

Pass by a gate and a bridge to the left to a gate in the wooden fence ahead. Go through the gate and continue in the same general direction to the right of the stream, to another gate in another wooden fence ahead. When you have gone through this, stick with the path until you approach a farm and the more distinct path slopes uphill towards it. Here stay parallel to the beck and aim for a gate between a barn and a crenellated wall. Go through the gate and follow a clear track to a gate to the right of a small stone building.

Climb through the stile to the left of the gate, cross the road and go through the stile across the road. Keeping in the same general direction, aim for a gap stile in the stone wall about 200 yards ahead. Go through this and follow the just visible path to a stile 100 yards ahead – perhaps 20 yards to the left of a gate. After negotiating the geriatric gate follow the hawthorn hedge on the right ahead. Birstwith Hall is visible to the left below. At the end of the field go through a gate into a green lane.

After 50 yards pass through another gate to a metalled driveway. Walk ahead along this to a road and turn right by a small green. Walk along this road uphill past a lane end to the left, Back Lane, and 50 yards further on look for a stile in the left hand wall on the corner where the road curves right. It is between two trees and may be hidden behind some rank herbage. Once in the field follow the left hand wall uphill along a just discernible footpath. It is worth stopping to look across at the extensive views to the right. On a good day you can see across the Vale of York to the Yorkshire Wolds.

As the fence curves leftwards follow it to aim for a ladder stile over a short length of crenellated wall in the far left corner of the field. Once over the stile pass between two trees through the largest of the many gaps in the hedge ahead and make for a gate in the barbed wire fence ahead. Now walk across the next field, aiming for a point roughly midway between a barn and a substantial house. As you near the wall you will see a stile in the corner of the field. Having negotiated this awkward stile turn right along the road.

You should now be able to see the pyramidal tower of Swarcliffe Hall for the first time, above and behind a cluster

The river Nidd at Birstwith, beside which Charlotte would have walked on her way to church.

of farms and houses. Pass three houses on the right and turn left opposite the fourth, a pink-washed Georgian farmhouse. Pass through a gate and immediately fork left in front of an attractive ivy-covered cottage. (The fork to the right is the driveway of Swarcliffe Hall.) Walk up to a gate and pass through a gate-stile to its right and then follow the wall uphill. The fine old brick wall visible across the orchard to your right is the boundary wall of Swarcliffe Hall's gardens. At the top of the field go through a gate and head for the stone house which seemingly blocks the way ahead. As you come up to it you will find a gate in the wall to the right. Go through this and turn left through the farm buildings. Once you are out of the farm buildings leave the track and cross a small piece of grass to a stile in the stone wall on its far side. Cross over and make for a gate visible to the left of two sets of stone buildings. Go through the gate and turn right along the road enjoying the first class views across the valley and into upper Nidderdale. On a good day Great Whernside will be visible on the horizon to the north west.

Pass by a reservoir in the fields below and a footpath, both on the right, and a large renovated farmhouse on the left and when you reach a farm on the left adjacent to the road, turn right along a good track posted 'Nidderdale Way'. From now on you will be following the Nidderdale Way all the way back to Hampsthwaite. Walk down this good track and continue straight ahead at a first gate across the track. However, at a second gate, immediately before a house, go through the gate, walk 20 yards and then strike off to the right along a path posted by a 'Nidderdale Way' sign. After a few yards this will bring you into a pleasant piece of ancient deciduous woodland.

Go downhill through this keeping close to the wall on the right. There is a clear path. Pass by a gate on the right and walk on to the bottom of the wood. Here go through a kissing gate into a field, then continue to follow the wall on your right to the bottom of the field. Cross the step stile to the right of the gate and turn right along the road. In spite of the usual sensible advice about facing the oncoming traffic there is something to be said in this case for walking on the left hand side of the road. You will be more visible and the verge is broader and easier to walk on. After about 250 yards, turn off down the first lane on your left along the route marked by the 'Nidderdale Way' sign. When the metalled lane comes to an end take the path ahead between the attractive mullioned-windowed 17th century farmhouse and its farm buildings.

When you see the arched packhorse bridge ahead do not cross it, but turn right over a stile. There should be another 'Nidderdale Way' sign. Follow the clear path to the right of the wooden fence to another stile, cross over this and continue straight ahead. The fence will now be to your right. The extensive parkland on the hillside above you to your right belongs to Swarcliffe Hall. Cross another stile and continue along the left hand edge of the field. As you approach the next fence you will find the stile to the left of an impressive tree. Cross over and walk along the right hand fence ahead. If you stop from time to time you will get interesting and changing glimpses of Swarcliffe Hall through the trees.

Hampsthwaite church in Nidderdale which Charlotte attended when employed by the Sidgwick family.

Cross two stiles in turn and walk along the left hand edge of a playing field. The village of Birstwith with its church is visible to the right, Birstwith Mills ahead. At the end of the playing field, cross the stile and stop to take in the view of Swarcliffe Hall. This is the best view of the house. Some of what you see would have been built when Charlotte was here with the Sidgwicks in 1839. However, there were alterations and extensions in 1848 and 1866–7.

After viewing the hall keep to the left hand side of the car park and go through a stile into the road. Now cross the road and following the 'Nidderdale Way' sign walk with some care between the buildings. When you meet another road you will see a footpath sign (and a 'Nidderdale Way' sign) pointing to a gate and a kissing gate. Go through and follow the left hand wall until you come to a slightly awkward stile in the far left hand corner. Here you will see a sign warning you that there is a bull in the field.

I have been through the field several times and have never encountered the animal concerned, despite the fact that last time I was here I combed the field looking for it. (It is in any case illegal to put a dairy bull, the dangerous sort, in a field crossed by a public footpath.) Taking your life in your hands then, set out across this extensive but pleasant pasture, wandering along the clearly visible path as it meanders its way 20 or so feet above the river. At the far end of the field cross a stile just to the right of the river and start along a similar meandering path. However, when you see some fenced round enclosures to your left ahead curve right uphill to a gate and kissing gate. Go through this into the road. It seems possible Charlotte used the path along the river side to go to and from Hampsthwaite Church. It is certain that she used the next section of the route.

Turn left along the road. This time it is better to walk on the right hand side of the road. Cross over the bridge across Tang Beck and just before the Hampsthwaite sign turn left by the seat and follow the footpath back through the churchyard to your car.

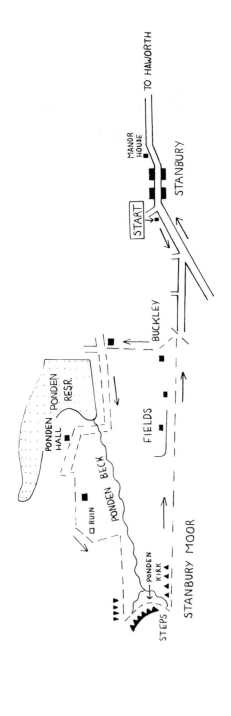

7

Ponden Hall: Thrushcross Grange of 'Wuthering Heights?'

Walking Distance: 5 miles

The two most prominent Trustees of Haworth Parish Church in Mr Brontë's time were Stephen Taylor of Stanbury and Robert Heaton of Ponden. We begin from Stanbury, have a look at the Manor House and the little church, where Mr Brontë preached, then take a route often used by Mr Brontë out to Buckley. From here we descend the hillside and walk up to Ponden Hall, a house certainly visited by Mr Brontë, Branwell and Emily and often regarded as the original of Thrushcross Grange of *Wuthering Heights*. We then return by Ponden Kirk, the scene of the huge Crow Hill 'eruption' and perhaps the original Brontë waterfall. We then return by a route commanding good views of this upper part of the Worth valley.

Stanbury and Stanbury Moor have been repeatedly associated with the Brontës. It was the received wisdom that if Top Withens was Wuthering Heights, Ponden Hall must be Thrushcross Grange. It was the right distance away from the Top Withens, roughly the right number of feet below and it was visibly much more of a gentleman's house than the Withens ever was. But the theory will not wash. Even if Ellen was right when she told George Smith that Emily had the location of Top Withens in mind when she created her Wuthering Heights, Ponden Hall could still never have been Thrushcross Grange. It had no gatehouse and no such extensive park as the Grange had. From the descriptions of it in the book, the Grange was a large Georgian country house with the typical rectangular windows of its kind – the sort of house more common in the Vale of York and East Yorkshire than around Haworth. More recently a spirited case has been made out that Ponden Hall was the original for Wuthering Heights itself. And certainly there are some affinities between the two houses' interiors. However, the exterior of the house in the novel is nothing like that of Ponden Hall: it is far closer to that of the now demolished High Sunderland Hall high on its bluff above Halifax. The truth is surely that Emily took bits and pieces of houses and geography – and perhaps people – from all over the Pennines and Yorkshire and created a new reality out of these. It is what Charlotte admitted that she did herself, when she created her characters.

So how did Stanbury and Ponden fit into the lives of the Brontës? The answer is simple. Without the intervention of Mr Taylor, the squire of Stanbury, whose descendants still live in the village, Mr Brontë would not have come to Haworth at all. The story is the usual mixture of small highlighted detail and large obscure gaps. However, amongst Patrick and Maria Brontë's closest friends at Thornton were the Kayes of Allerton Hall. Mercy Kaye was a close relative of the Taylors of Stanbury, no fewer than four of whom were among the Trustees of Haworth Church. So whilst we have no proof, it seems as good as certain that it was this family connection that eased the path of Mr Brontë when he proposed to move to Haworth. After Patrick took up his post there in 1820 he would have had to pay regular visits to both the Taylors of Stanbury and the other leading Stanbury family, the Heatons of Ponden. As both families contained Trustees of the Church and were relatively wealthy, this was essential. All the more so as both families, it now seems, were far from being totally committed to the Church. Both oddly were equally anxious to keep one foot in the Methodist camp – each paying out money for a small chapel of its own. The Taylors, primarily a farming family, were involved in Stanbury's new Methodist chapel; the Heatons, a more entrepre-

Looking towards Stanbury from Haworth Moor, where Emily used to walk.

neurial family, who ran quarries, a small coal mine, a cotton mill and a corn mill as well as farming, were just as involved with the rival Scar Top Chapel, about a mile west of Stanbury.

So how did the Brontës get on with these two rival dynasties? Surprisingly in the light of the tons of material written about the Brontës, very much better with the Taylors. There is no comparison between the letters written to the Heatons and those to the Taylors. Such letters to the Heatons as survive are business-like to the point of brusqueness; there is a much more relaxed and intimate tone in the letters to the Taylors. In fact the Taylors would seem to have been the nearest equivalent at Haworth to the Firth family and Kaye family at Thornton. Aunt Branwell, a figure curiously neglected by many biographers, was no small part of this. Thus in a letter to George Taylor of 6 June 1832, Mr Brontë adds: 'Miss Branwell joins me in kind regards.' On 30 April 1833 she showed this regard by making the same George Taylor one of the three executors of her will. The same quiet friendliness was to continue. In approximately 1844 Charlotte invited Mrs Taylor to tea to meet a Mr and Mrs Rand and a Miss Bacon. In probably the same year Mr Brontë also wrote to the Taylors gently suggesting that they invited Enoch Thomas, then suffering from acute depression, to tea. This was the sort of favour one would ask only of good friends, but then George Taylor and other Taylors were amongst the select few later to be invited to Charlotte's wedding. These were the Brontës' real friends in the Haworth area.

The contrast with the Heatons could not be more stark. There was no such involvement in pleasant family occasions here. By contrast with the pleasant correspondence with the Taylors, these missives are little more than business notes announcing dates for meetings and requesting their presence at them or passing on letters from the Vicar of Bradford which had to be discussed at meetings. Now of course it is possible that the surviving correspondence misrepresents the relationship. It so happens that the list of books in the old Ponden Hall library survives and on the basis of one or two titles which seem to have caught the eyes of the young Brontës some leading scholars have argued strongly that the Brontës must have used the library. However this is probably not so. In depth study of quotations in the children's juvenilia and mature writings strongly suggests the reverse – that the Brontës' literary interests started at the date at which the latest books in the Heaton library had been published. There is more evidence in fact that if there was any socialising it was because of the Heatons' extensive sporting estate on Stanbury Moor. Mr Brontë was to mention in a letter to Lord John Manners that he had been a good shot and we are fairly certain Branwell was to continue the family tradition. In fact one passage in his voluminous unpublished writings explicitly mentions Ponden, whilst another sporting passage is clearly set in Ponden Kirk, but that said, we would be safer to assume that the relationship was largely a functional one. Both the older Heatons and the younger Heatons were the wrong ages for there to be any close friendship between the young Brontës and themselves.

However there is one possible exception to this lack of contact. If, as an early local tradition believed and one or two early books on the area also agreed, the mysterious 'Brontë waterfall' was not where it is now believed to be, but at the head of the Ponden valley, then it is as good as certain that that great fell-walker Emily would regularly have made her way by Ponden Hall to go and visit it. And, interestingly, there was a tradition amongst the Heatons that Robert Heaton had actually planted a pear tree for Emily, whilst another separate tradition reported that Emily was the only one of the Brontës that the family had known at all well. Oddly enough then there might have been a link between *Wuthering Heights*, the novel, and Ponden Hall after all. Could Emily's picture of Nelly browsing upstairs at Thrushcross Grange amongst the old books have been a portrait of herself left to her own devices amongst the books – also upstairs – at Ponden Hall? A local writer, Mary Butterfield, also draws attention to the anagrammatic closeness of Hareton and Heaton. Given other local echoes in the names, it is the sort of detail that would have appealed to Emily.

THE WALK OVER STANBURY MOOR TO PONDEN HALL

Parking in Stanbury is a bit of a problem. It is often possible at the west end of the village where there is a small patch of green between two roads. If this is not available you could park on the main street or, with the permission of the licensee, in the large car park adjacent to the Wuthering Heights inn.

Wherever you park it is worth walking back through Stanbury. This was part of Mr Brontë's 'parish' when he was at Haworth. Almost at the end of the village you will see the Manor House on the left. In the time of the Brontës the Taylors lived here who, as trustees of Haworth Church, were

Stanbury Manor House, home of the Taylor family, friends of the Brontës at Haworth.

instrumental in getting the living for Mr Brontë. One of their descendants still lives in the house. Turn back and pass the Wuthering Heights pub on the right. Facing it is the old Wesleyan chapel – now converted into housing. This was first built here in 1832, but it attracted so much support it was expanded on two later occasions. Interestingly enough, members of the Taylor family were also amongst the trustees of this place of worship. In the Haworth area at least some families seem to have made a habit of attending the services of more than one denomination.

Walk past the Friendly Inn on the right. The Anglican church a little further on, on the same side, was built in the late 1840s – presumably to counteract the growing popularity of the chapel. If you look inside – a villager will tell you where you can obtain a key – you will see the old pulpit from Haworth Parish Church in which Mr Brontë used to preach. (It must be said, however, that there is little other reason to look in the church, which is now used as a community centre as well as a church.)

When you reach the fork in the road take the left fork slightly uphill. After about 300 yards fork right along a lane signposted Buckley Green and Ponden Kirk. Pass three farm buildings on the right. Where the lane divides into three take the middle one signposted Pennine Way and Brontë Way. Just before the next farm go through a stile on the right – again signposted Pennine Way and Brontë Way – and follow first an enclosed path and later a track down to a lane. Turn left here and walk ahead with Ponden Reservoir to your right.

When the lane curves uphill follow it. Do not go left to the farm or Ponden Centre. Walk uphill to Ponden Hall which has been variously associated with Thrushcross Grange and Wuthering Heights. During the time of the Brontës the Heatons lived here, who were also trustees of Haworth Church (and great supporters of Scar Top Methodist Chapel, the local rival to Stanbury Chapel!) It has been suggested that the Brontës borrowed books from the extensive library here. (The date above the door incidentally refers to the last 'facelift' the building had, not the date at which it was originally built.)

After looking at Ponden Hall walk ahead through buildings. After 200 yards past the hall fork left. Walk uphill past the entrance to another farm. When you pass through a gate on to the open moor, keep to the right hand wall as directed by signs. When the wall comes to an end walk 100 yards ahead to a fork, footpath signs and a 'Private' notice. Here turn left and walk along a narrow but clear path towards a ruined wall to the right of a deserted farm building. There are posts to indicate the way. As you come up to the wall go through the gap to the right of where two ruined walls meet.

Follow the ruined wall on your left hand side ahead until you meet a broad track. Turn right along this and walk towards the head of the valley. When you reach a broad gravel parking area follow the signpost's direction and walk down to the lower path on the left. Some local traditions have maintained that the cascade which you are now approaching was the original Brontë Waterfall. Before the abstraction installations were built it was almost certainly a more impressive sight than the present favourite for that title. Go down the steps and crossing warily, walk below the water abstraction installation to pick up the path on the far side.

Now walk ahead, contouring round the head of the valley to another water abstraction plant. Climb up the steps on the right. There is a good handrail on the left, but take care on the steps. At the top cross the stream by a public footpath sign. Unless the beck is in spate there should be no problem. Now turn sharp left and follow the narrow path that contours above the crags towards a post on the skyline. Now keep on ahead at roughly the same height with open moor to your right and a ravine to your left. Posts reassuringly mark the way.

After 500 yards the path converges with a stone wall. Walk parallel with this for 300 yards. When you reach a garden full of willows − 'withens' − cross the stile and walk down the wallside to the track. Turn right along the track. Where the Pennine Way and Brontë Way go right uphill, carry on straight ahead down into the farmyard of Buckley Green. When the Pennine Way and Brontë Way now turn downhill, again carry on in the same direction ahead. Turn left at the T-junction and then right at the main road. You are now back in Stanbury.

8

Branwell at Luddendenfoot

This figure of eight walk begins at the station where Branwell was employed as Clerk in Charge from April 1841 to March 1842. Sadly nothing at all of the station is left standing today. We follow the route by which he would have commuted to the Lord Nelson at Luddenden where he drank, met friends and read books. After a look round the pub and the church – where Grimshaw of Haworth is buried – we explore in turn the east and west sides of Luddenden Dean. Both of these roads were probably used by Branwell on his way to and from home between April and July 1841. After encircling the upper valley we return over the hills by a route which commands a panoramic view of Calderdale as a whole, an area that Branwell explored extensively during his period at Sowerby Bridge and Luddendenfoot.

'A distant relative of mine, one Patrick Boarnerges, has set off to seek his fortune in the wild, wandering, adventurous, romantic, knight-errant-like capacity of clerk on the Leeds and Manchester Railroad. Leeds and Manchester, where are they? Cities in a wilderness – like Tadmor, alias Palmyra – are they not?'

So Charlotte wrote to Ellen on 29 September 1840. Branwell's motivation for taking a position with the railway company was to earn some money and also give himself the chance to meet up regularly with his artistic and literary friends in Halifax. It also shows that at this stage, at least, Branwell was not one to shirk any reasonable job.

For this job he was to be paid £75 a year – payment of £18.15.0 to be made at the end of every quarter. For this he had to name two sureties – for a sum of £210 – in the event his father and aunt. So at the end of September, a few days

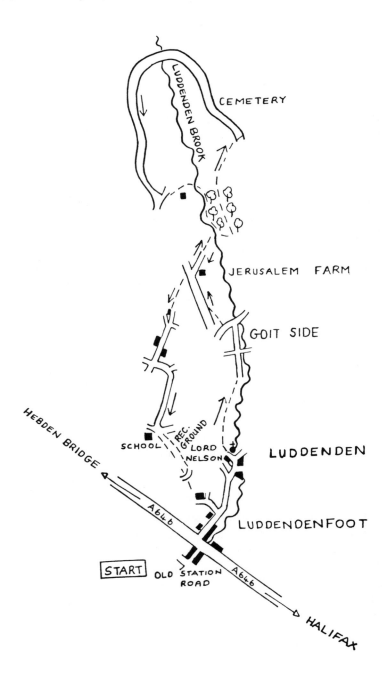

before the opening of the railway from Leeds to Hebden Bridge, Branwell took up his post as Assistant Clerk in Charge at Sowerby Bridge and went into lodgings with a family called Bates who owned a beer house on the steep Sowerby Street (later to be called The Pear Tree Inn). It may seem an appropriate place to stay, but Sowerby Bridge had a number of good hostelries, The Bull's Head, The Royal Oak and The Wharfe. And Branwell is reputed to have frequented all of them!

His work at Sowerby Bridge was probably tiring rather than hard. And there is some evidence that he had enough energy after and between work to walk over to Halifax to meet his numerous friends and that they also came down to Sowerby Bridge to see him. Two of the most important were the Leyland brothers. Joseph Leyland, most of whose work has now vanished, was a wild, blasphemous sculptor, who produced sculpture in what one might call the new Romantic idiom. His brother Francis was a quiet, sedate, scholarly figure. We are privileged to have Francis's first impressions of Branwell:

'It was on a bright Sunday afternoon in the autumn of 1840, at the desire of my brother, the sculptor, that I accompanied him to the station at Sowerby Bridge to see Branwell. The young railway clerk was of gentleman-like appearance and seemed to be qualified for a much better position than the one he had chosen. In stature he was a little below the middle height; not 'almost insignificantly small', as Mr Grundy states, nor had he 'a downcast look': neither was he 'a plain specimen of humanity.' He was very slim and agile in figure, yet of well-formed outline. His complexion was clear and ruddy, and the expression of his face, at the time, lightsome and cheerful. His voice had a ringing sweetness, and the utterance and use of his English was perfect: Branwell appeared to be in excellent spirits, and showed none of those traces of intemperance with which some writers have unjustly credited him about this period of his life.'

Leyland's comments about his sobriety seem to be borne

out. It seems clear he performed well in this first job. And on 1 April 1841 he was promoted to the new station at Ludden-denfoot, two miles further up the valley to be Clerk in Charge at the vastly increased salary of £130 per annum. As Char-lotte wrote a little apprehensively to Emily (who had obviously heard from him): 'It is to be hoped that his removal to another station will turn out for the best. As you say, it *looks* like getting on at any rate.'

At Luddendenfoot Branwell was to meet yet another friend who was always to remember him, Francis Grundy. It is also worth quoting his strikingly different recollections: Branwell was 'almost insignificantly small. He had a mass of red hair, which he wore brushed high on his forehead, nearly half the size of his whole facial contour; small ferrety eyes, deep, sunk, and still further hidden by the never removed specta-cles; prominent nose, but weak lower features. He had a downcast look, which never varied, save for a rapid momen-tary glance at long intervals. Small and thin of person, he was the reverse of attractive at first sight.'

Grundy is a valuable source. Unreliable as he is, he com-ments cogently on Branwell's love of good conversation, his craze on foreign quotations (which he then always trans-lated). More interestingly he shows that Branwell was any-thing but lonely, but knew 'plenty of wild, rollicking, hard-headed half-educated manufacturers, who would welcome him to their houses, and drink with him as often as he chose to come'.

This socialising probably became more compulsive the longer he stayed. Grundy, who saw him as someone 'who couldn't bear to be alone' and full of 'eagerness for excite-ment' suggests that his absences without leave 'carousing with congenial drinkers' started to be 'of days' continuance'. He was plainly a great local favourite. This does not neces-sarily mean that he neglected his job. Even some of the lines of the poems that he compulsively continued to write show that he was not always off duty even when being creative:

'I ... sat amid
The bustle of a town-like room
Neath skies, with smoke stain'd vapours hid –
By windows, made to show their gloom.
The desk that held my ledger book
Beneath the thundering rattle shook
Of engines passing by ...'

If when he was dismissed there was considerable local pressure to get him reinstated, it was certainly not because he was a likeable rogue, but because he was courteous, helpful and on the whole conscientious. Sentimentality is the last word that springs to mind about Yorkshire woollen manufacturers.

No, what was to cause his downfall was not his sociability, but something else entirely. Having read through Branwell's schoolwork and the Luddendenfoot Notebook I strongly suspect that his Achilles heel was arithmetic. (It seems strange otherwise that it was the girls – and especially Emily – who looked after the family's accounts.) In any event Leyland tells us, after several 'unwelcome enquiries and remonstrances', Branwell was called before the company to account for an imbalance in the books of £11.1.7d. He could not do so and when his books were examined – these would be the ledgers – the margins were found to be covered with doodles. However this was not the crucial point, but the financial slovenliness. The amount short was deducted, therefore, from his salary and Branwell was sacked (although the ticket collector often thought to be the cause of Branwell's woes was retained). This was not quite the end of Branwell at Luddendenfoot. Company records show that several local merchants and millowners interceded strongly on his behalf, asking that he be reinstated. It came to nothing, but it does prove that Branwell must have been more use at his job than is often thought.

The friendships that Branwell built up whilst in Calderdale were to continue too. It is not generally realised that Branwell was the first of the Brontës to be published commercially.

The centre of Luddenden village, where Branwell spent so much of his time whilst at Luddendenfoot.

Starting on 5 June 1841 the *Halifax Guardian* was to publish six of Branwell's poems (and other local newspapers were to follow). Less beneficially, Halifax and its environs became a sort of asylum to which he bolted when life got too much for him. He took to haunting one of the most prestigious pubs in Halifax – and one that still survives – the Old Cock Inn. Here rubbing shoulders with Freemasons of the Lodge of Probity, the local Whigs, the musicians of the New Harmonic Society, the merchants and millowners who came to the Piece Hall, he was to spend both time and money, impressing others no doubt with his fluent conversation, still perhaps executing his lightning sketches. Finally the whole thing came to a series of rather sad heads: firstly in early December 1846 when the landlord of the Old Cock, Thomas Nicholson, sent a Sheriff's Officer over to Haworth to demand payment of the vast debts that Branwell had run up; secondly on 22 July 1848 when a letter from Branwell to Joseph Leyland shows that not only was Nicholson threatening another summons, but he had been joined by Mrs Sugden of *The Talbot* who was also demanding a settling of accounts. It was the old Luddendenfoot trouble again – living beyond his means trying to cut an impressive figure amongst his friends. This time though he was faced with something worse even than the sack – gaol!

THE WALK AROUND LUDDENDEN DEAN

This walk is a figure of eight. There is parking both at the start of the walk and half way round, where the two loops meet. So it is possible to do it as two smaller circular walks or as one long one.

A. If doing the whole of the walk or the first part only, turn off the A646 Halifax–Burnley road in the middle of Luddendenfoot (pronounced 'London-foot'). The turning will be on your left if you are coming from Halifax; on your right if you are coming from Hebden Bridge. It is not signposted to anywhere but it is the old road to the railway station at which Branwell Brontë worked for twelve months in 1841–2. Park your car on either Station Road itself or on Old Station Road.

There is now no trace of the old railway station left. The walk, however, follows routes by which Branwell walked to and from his favourite pub in the area and also to and from home. (In those days rights of way allowed walkers to walk up to the very head of the Luddenden valley and then, by routes that have still not been extinguished, down into Oxenhope.) Walk down Station Road to the main road. Turn left, cross the road and in a few yards turn right, up Luddenden Lane. Walk uphill past the attractive Kershaw House on the left, a fine example of a Halifax House, as the style is called. Just past the toilet block on the right turn right down High Street into the old village of Luddenden.

Keep right over the bridge, then to the left of the Luddenden Club building. Go past the Post Office and at the next turn go left through High Street Fold. Just after the bridge you will see the attractive Lord Nelson inn on your left. This is where Branwell spent much of his leisure time whilst at Luddendenfoot. As well as the ales and the food, it offered a good library upstairs. Both the pub and the church opposite are worth a visit. If Branwell was still going to church at this time this would have been the one he would have attended.

Now take the footpath to the west – left – of the church. Walk along the riverside past Brook Terrace. (Unusually for Yorkshire, the river is called Luddenden Brook.) Pass by an impressive Victorian house and its Gothic 'garage'. Keep straight ahead past some more cottages on to a metalled lane to enter the hamlet of Goit Side. When you reach a main road turn left and walk uphill. Just opposite to a large building on the left – the old school – turn right up some steps and walk up the field, following the wall on the right hand side to some more steps in the top right hand corner of the field. Climb the steps and go through the wooden gate and turn right into Jerusalem Lane. Walk for about 300 yards to Jerusalem Farm on the right.

Here you have two choices. If you wish to explore the upper part of the valley continue with **Section B**. If you wish to return to Luddendenfoot at this point turn to **Section C**.

B. If you only wish to visit the upper part of Luddenden Dean there is a good car park just past Jerusalem Farm on the right. There should be no problem parking except perhaps at weekends and in the height of summer.

Walk down the lane through the car park to Wade Bridge at the bottom of the hill. Cross the brook and turn right. Look for the higher of two footpaths and follow it uphill through the trees. When you meet another footpath descending from the left, turn sharp left. There is a small unobtrusive 'Calderdale Way' sign pointing the way. Now wind gradually uphill through the trees. Ignore a footpath on the right climbing steeply uphill to Saltonstall. Continue steadily uphill. Eventually you will reach a wall coming up from the left. Keep on its right hand side until you come to a large gateway and extensively barbed wired gate. There is a gap stile just beyond this to admit you to a green track on the other side of the wall. Follow this lane increasingly steeply uphill. As you reach a building, The Hullett, (West Yorkshire for Owlet), you will find a gate to its left. Go through this and walk up first grass and then a driveway to a metalled road, Heys Lane. Turn left.

Walk for about a ⅓ mile along this quiet lane until you come to a cemetery on the right. This is all that remains of Luddenden Dean Chapel built 1828. It is worth looking out for the 'Orphans' Grave' facing the road between the two gates. It records the deaths of seven orphan girls aged between 12 and 17 who worked for a nearby textile firm, I. I. Calvert of Wainstalls. Interestingly for the background of *Wuthering Heights*, we know that later in the 19th century the firm got some of its young girl employees from Liverpool.

Leave the cemetery and walk past the obtrusively restored Nunnery to the bottom of the hill, cross the bridge and walk past the entrance to the Castle Carr estate on the right. This is ferociously barbed wired against all intruders, but in the time of the Brontës rights of way ran through the estate to the head of the valley and climbed up to the High road to Oxenhope. With what legality I know not, these were all extinguished in the late 19th century. So walk through the impressive castellated gatehouse and follow the road south along the other side of the valley.

Continue along this road when it turns into a sandy lane. Follow this lane until you come to a gateway with a gate across the road and immediately to its left beyond it another gate into a private driveway. There may be a sign saying 'Upper Mytholm'. Just behind the second gate you will see on your left in the trees a small footbridge across a beck. Cross this and follow the path between the beck and a right hand fence to a stile. Cross the stile and follow the left hand fence downhill to a small gate. Keeping the stream on your left aim first for a small wooden stile and then across a field to a footbridge visible at the edge of the woods ahead.

Cross the footbridge and follow the clear path ahead below the hillside. You will come to two steeper escarpments above the river. At the first keep below the cliffs and walk along the rocks beside the brook (unless, of course, the brook is in flood). As you approach the second, however, you will find it blocked by an intimidating grid-shaped fence. Here take any of the slanting paths uphill to a gate and a stile above the escarpment. Cross into the woodland and follow the clear path back to Wade Bridge and the car park at Jerusalem Farm.

C. If returning to Luddendenfoot walk on the road until you are opposite Jerusalem Farm. Take the footpath into the field on the right and climb uphill at an angle half right to the road below. Climb up to a stile and continue in the same direction to a gap and a post in a ruined wall ahead. Go through this and cross another ruined wall on your right. Now make uphill to the far right hand corner of the field in front. The footpath is mostly clear to follow. Go through the stile at the top and follow the right hand wall ahead. Cross another stile and then follow the wall as it curves right to a farm gate.

Enter the yard and walk past a line of terraced houses into a gravel lane. Ignore a turn downhill on the left. When you join a metalled road, High House Lane, walk ahead. Keep straight ahead at the same level until you have passed two lines of terraced houses. Then, when you reach a crossroads of roads and paths turn left down a walled lane, the first length of which is cobbled. When the cobbles come to an end turn right along a walled path.

Walk ahead ignoring paths off to the left and right. When the path comes to an end opposite a school, turn left past houses and a shop. In about 150 yards you will see a lane, Green Lane, off to the right of an unusually shaped house. Walk down this past a recreation ground to a stile. Cross the stile and walk straight ahead along a right hand fence. (There

Luddenden churchyard. This is a view Branwell would often have had from the Lord Nelson Inn. And if he still went to church at that time, this would have been the church he would have attended.

are sometimes cattle in this field, but they are less frightening than they look.) When you reach the bottom of the field go through the stile and veer right. Ignore a good track coming up from the left. Go through a gateway and follow a wall on the left until it bends left. Just beyond the corner of this wall you will find a footpath going downhill between two stone walls. Follow it down to the bottom and descend some stone steps into a field.

Walk down the field following a right hand wall. At the bottom go through a stile and walk between the buildings into Kershaw Drive. Walk down Kershaw Drive to Ludden-den Lane, turn right and in 300 yards you will find yourself back at Burnley Road, the A646. Station Road is a few yards away to your left on the far side.

9

Thorp Green
And 'The Tenant of Wildfell Hall'

Walking Distance: 4¼ miles

We begin from the village in which Anne went to church every Sunday, Little Ouseburn Church, pass by the church, which she drew, and pass round the perimeter of a house, Kirby Hall, which she would have visited. On our way round we go through the Long Plantation, where she wrote one of her poems, to go as close to the river Ouse as we are allowed. Branwell liked to sit here. We then ramble into Thorpe Underwood, the Thorp Green of the Brontës, pass the house in which Branwell stayed and return to Little Ouseburn along the route by which Anne and the Robinsons would have gone to and from church.

Almost everything about Thorp Green's involvement with the Brontë family is a mystery. We do not know how Anne contacted – or was contacted by – the Robinsons; how she travelled from Haworth to Thorp Green; when she first took up her duties; why she continued to work there though she was obviously sometimes unhappy; what sort of people the Robinsons were – and Mrs Robinson, in particular; what really went on between Branwell and the Robinsons to lead to his summary dismissal.

The Robinson family was a much more upper class family than Anne had come into contact with before. A traditional country landowner, the Rev Edmund Robinson had grown up in the area and in his twenties married Lydia Gisborne, youngest child of a wealthy Evangelical clergyman, Thomas Gisborne. There is some slight evidence of antipathy between

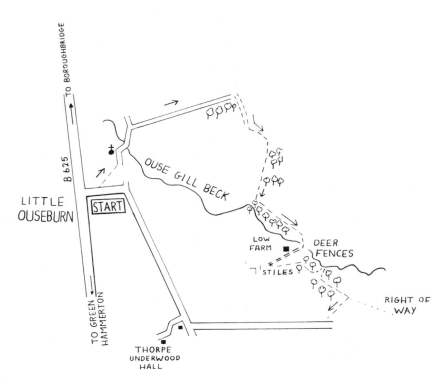

the two families, but there is no need to suppose that this poisoned the relationship between Edmund and Lydia themselves. The couple had five children; Edmund kept Lydia in style; both played a complementary part in local life; both referred on occasion to the other with affection. The couple were, in fact, locally popular and seem not to have stood on ceremony. The sincere affection felt is shown by comments in the diary of a local man, George Whitehead. So when young Lydia Robinson eloped with Henry Roxby in October 1845, he described it as a 'bad job', the very same phrase he was to use when the Robinsons left the area altogether in early March 1847. Perhaps the crowning proof of Mr Robinson's popularity is that no fewer than 60 Oddfellows followed his cortege when he was buried.

It was into this old-fashioned environment that Anne first

came in 1841 – or possibly 1840 – to act as governess. Both her Diary Paper and her poetry strongly suggest she was far from happy at the move and anxious to leave as soon as possible. Obviously in part this may have been something to do with the Robinsons, but the unprecedented distance from home and Emily, in particular, must also have played their part. At this distance and at this period there was virtually no chance of visits either way. That said, the Robinsons would seem to have treated her very liberally, given the attitudes of the time. Perhaps from the very start Anne went with them on the trips to York which we know they took; she certainly accompanied them on their extended visits to Scarborough, then at the very height of fashion, and there she would have met and perhaps mingled with the numerous other wealthy people and their 'dependants' who visited the resort during the season. If Mr Robinson himself was increasingly dyspeptic, there seems every indication that the family were happy to treat Anne as one of themselves. The best proof of this comes from later on, in the lost correspondence between the Robinsons and Anne and the visits the girls paid her when she was back in Haworth. There is no need to think that this friendship had not begun a lot earlier. In fact it seems as good as certain that it was because of their respect for Anne that they decided to take Branwell on, too, as tutor to their son, Edmund. It was a grave misjudgement.

For his part, Branwell must have leapt at the invitation. His career as a painter had long since ended in failure and there was no possibility of returning to the railway. After the successive débâcles of the last several years he must have felt as though he had landed on his feet. He was not merely to be housed in luxurious style and to associate with the rich and privileged, he was now to have the opportunity to show off his many-sided talents as a part of his job. He now at last found himself in a family who loved and performed good music, who borrowed and read up-to-date books from the circulating libraries of York, who sketched and perhaps painted, who were only too anxious for their slightly back-

Thorpe Underwood Hall as it is today. It was built on the site of Thorp Green Hall, the home of the Robinson family, where Anne and Branwell were employed in the early 1840s.

ward son to acquire the Classical accomplishments which were a *sine qua non* of a young Victorian gentleman. He seemed to possess all these skills in one. The family's gratitude and appreciation were unbounded. In Branwell's first year at Thorp Green Mr Brontë himself was invited over to the house to stay for a few days. During this visit relations between the Robinsons could only have been on the basis of friendship rather than of employer to employee. And it is hard to see them being at any other level after Mr Brontë's departure. It seems likely that Charlotte was reporting Mr Brontë's own verdict when later on she was to write to Ellen: 'Anne and Branwell ... are both wondrously valued in their situations.' It must have seemed to both of them, but especially to Branwell, that his wildest dreams had come true. One fulfilling activity followed another – long walks with Edmund, drawing with Lydia, holidays on the coast, visits to the theatre ... so what went wrong?

Obviously there has been a lot of speculation. One thing can, I think, be stated for certain – it did concern Branwell's relations with Mrs Robinson. The infatuation is all the easier to understand and to forgive because of Mr Robinson's well-attested testiness and the divergence of interests between husband and wife. As for Branwell, the appeal of a highly cultured, refined, sophisticated and above all wealthy woman – even one so much older than himself – hardly needs to be spelled out. The doodles, the spelling out of Lydia's name both in English and in Greek alongside poems written long after, all confirm the genuineness of the feeling.

What happened physically we can only speculate. 'Something bad beyond expression' can mean different things to different people. The subsequent outraged moral attitudes of the Robinsons has suggested to many that they had nothing to hide. It seems possible also that Branwell may have made more of a fairly routine upper-class 'flirtation' than he was meant to. A born fantasist, he had been churning out novelet-tish stories of upper class seductions since his adolescence. What more natural than that he should interpret what was happening within terms of these?

The end of the affair is as hard to sort out as the beginning of Anne's stay at Thorp Green. Usually Anne and Branwell would have gone home for a short summer break and then rejoined the Robinsons on their way to or at Scarborough. In Anne's case there is no problem. On 11 June she was paid off; her job was completed. Branwell, too, was paid on the same day, Mr Robinson's entry-book recording that this was the salary that was 'due July 21st', the word July being under-lined. However hardly had Branwell reached home than he told Charlotte that he had to return to Thorp Green within the week. Still more confusingly he also told her that he would return to Haworth when the Robinsons went to Scarborough. It seems certain Charlotte believed this. So how about Anne? Either she knew it was a lie – in which case she was Branwell's accomplice – or she too believed it. Neither seems easy to take. And the same is true of Branwell's behaviour. Some scholars have seen this as an elaborate charade on Branwell's part, but it is hard to square this with the complete physical and emotional collapse which came when he *did* know he was dismissed. The assumption that he was telling the truth is hardly less problematic. Why was he not to go to Scarborough? I am inclined to think that Mr Robinson's payment was merely a payment in advance, not a pay-off. Branwell was never able to handle money. Perhaps the easiest solution is that Branwell was meant to look after Edmund until he went to Scarborough and that when Edmund reached Scarborough – perhaps late – he innocently blurted out what had been going on between his mother and Branwell. The boy's naivety is attested by his next tutor, the Rev Theophilous Williams of Charlton Mackwell in Somerset.

In any event the result was the same. Both Anne and Branwell were never to return to Thorp Green. Anne turned her experiences to good use. In due course, *Agnes Grey*, perhaps begun at Thorp Green, and *The Tenant of Wildfell Hall* followed.

THE WALK FROM LITTLE OUSEBURN TO THORPE UNDERWOOD

Park in Little Ouseburn off the B6265 (Green Hammerton to Boroughbridge road). There is room to park adjacent to the Village Hall, the former village school, on the right hand side of the street, the south side, about ½ mile off the main road. If this is full, it should be possible to park considerably on the street itself. Now with your back to the Village Hall cross the street to a kissing gate to the right of a house and its drive. Go through the kissing gate and go half right across the small field to another kissing gate in the hawthorn hedge over to the right. Pass through this kissing gate and turn left along the pavement on the near side of the road. You will soon see Little Ouseburn church ahead. This is the church which Anne Brontë – and presumably Branwell – attended when at Thorp

Little Ouseburn Church, which Anne attended while governess at Thorp Green Hall.

Green. Anne's drawings of the church and the bridge are in
the Brontë Parsonage Museum. Have a look round the
churchyard and the interesting church if open.

After leaving the church turn left on the left hand pavement
and walk down to the footbridge over Ouse Gill Beck. When
this small brook joins the river Ure a couple of miles down
stream the main river changes its name to the river Ouse.
Continue alongside the road to the T-junction ahead. Then
take the road to the right signposted 'Linton on Ouse',
Beningborough Hall and Aldwark (Toll Bridge)'. There is no
pavement along this road and it can be busy, but there is a
wide grass verge on the right. However, take care and watch
for the low electric wires in the trees just past the gates of
Kirby Hall on the right. Walk past a lane on the left with a
notice saying 'No Tipping Allowed' to just past the end of a
wood a few yards further on, on the right. Here turn right
through a large gate and proceed along a track.

Follow this to the end of the wood on your right hand side
and go through a gate into a field, still keeping to the track,
which is now along its left hand edge. When you reach
another gate the track ends. Here turn left for about 75 yards
to a gate and stile. Cross the stile and turn right. There is a
wire fence and later a hedge to your right. At the end of this
you will see a stile leading into a wood. Cross this and walk
through the wood keeping close to its right hand edge. There
is a vestigial path visible. Across the field beyond the hedge
you will see the outbuildings of Kirby Hall. The hall itself has
been demolished. There is a drawing of Flossie, also at the
Brontë Parsonage Museum, which may include it in the far
distance. At the end of the wood cross another stile into a
field. The right of way now goes half left across the field, but
there are often crops in the field and it is probably in
everyone's interest to follow the wire fence on the right
straight ahead to yet another wood ahead. When you reach
this wood turn left and follow its perimeter round to the
right.

As you approach the end of the wood you will see a series

of 7 foot high deer fences ahead. These may present some problems. If the gate into these is locked, walk down to the streamlet a few yards away to the right, Ouse Gill Beck again, and ford it and climb up the far side into the farmyard ahead. Walk through the farmyard and follow the track straight ahead for perhaps 75 yards to a redundant stile on the left hand side of the track. Here turn very sharp left so that you are almost going back the way you came. Follow the hedge on the right to another stile. Cross this and then go straight across a paddock to another stile. The next bit can be a little like an assault course. Climb three 7 foot high stiles in turn to enter a small newly planted wood. However, it is possible some of the gates may be open. If so cross the bridge by the track and once across it go through the gate immediately on the left. In the top left hand corner you will see a 7 foot high stile. Cross this into a small newly planted wood.

However you get there, you are now in the small newly planted wood. Keep to the right hand edge of this until you reach a rather denser wood and savage-looking barbed wire fence in front. Turn sharp left here and walk down beside the fence to reach Ouse Gill Beck yet again. Here you can get round the barbed wire fence and by climbing over or crawling under another easier piece of barbed wire make your way into the wood. Watch your step in this wood. The vegetation can be quite long and in places there are twigs and logs hidden away in all the foliage. Perhaps the simplest approach is to follow the sinister looking barbed wire fence back again and then turn left at the top for perhaps 300 yards. At the earliest available opportunity walk through the gappy hedge to your right into the field. Your troubles – or excitement – are now at an end.

Once in the field keep along the top side of the wood to yet another barbed wire fence. (They don't believe in letting the corn escape in North Yorkshire.) If you look carefully you will find a stile in its far left hand corner. Cross this and you will find yourself in a rough overgrown field. As it is not possible to follow the right of way as printed on the map, you

Anne Brontë's bridge. It seems likely she brought her young charges here to sketch. One of her drawings at the Brontë Parsonage Museum resembles the bridge.

have two choices. Neither, you will be relieved to know, is very difficult. One option is to follow the left hand hedge as it veers rightwards until you come to a gap between this hedge and another fence. You pass through this gap and follow the fence on your right to a corner and when it bends 90 degrees to the right continue to follow it to the hedge ahead. Here you will come to a gateway on the right. Go through this into a short fenced track to another gate. Climb over this and you will find you are on a good track at the right hand side of a field.

The other option once you have crossed the stile is to turn right and follow the right hand hedge to a gate. Go through this and almost instantly turn sharp left along what is often a clear track. Follow this for about 20 yards then turn half right and walk across the field to a fence and a gate ahead. There is often a track visible on the ground. When you reach this you will find yourself emerging into a field with an excellent track along its right edge. This is the same track as you reach by the alternative route.

At this point the right of way is supposed to head half left across the field to a corner between a wood and the hedge. And if you do this you will find there is an excellent stile there. However, it is often not possible to do this because of the crops grown in this field. If this is so, the best thing is to follow the good track on the right hand side of the field until it comes out at a metalled road. In any event, at whatever point you emerge into the road turn right for Thorpe Underwood, the village in which Thorp Green Hall was situated. Newly published poetry of Branwell's reveals that he used to come down this lane to sit by the river bank. Unfortunately, however, there is no right of access to the bank at this point. Having turned right, keep straight along this lane. Ignore two tracks off to the left and don't worry about the notices saying it is a private road. It is also a public footpath. After about a ⅓ mile you will find yourself in Thorpe Underwood. Until a few years ago the village looked something like it did in the time of the Brontës. Now with new walls everywhere and large developments it is almost impossible to imagine the way it was. However, if you follow the road round to the right you will pass by the Monks House where Branwell lived during his period of employment and if you turn sharp left at the T-junction just beyond this and walk for about 200 yards down to the left you will see the other side of the Monks House. If you proceed a little further to beyond Thorpe Underwood Hall and turn round you can get a good view of the house that replaced Thorp Green Hall when it was burnt down at the beginning of the 20th century.

When you have seen as much as you want to turn back to the T-junction and keep to the main road when the road by which you joined it comes in from the right. If you continue along this quiet road for about 1¼ miles you will come to Little Ouseburn. Here turn left and in a few yards you will see the Village Hall and its car park.

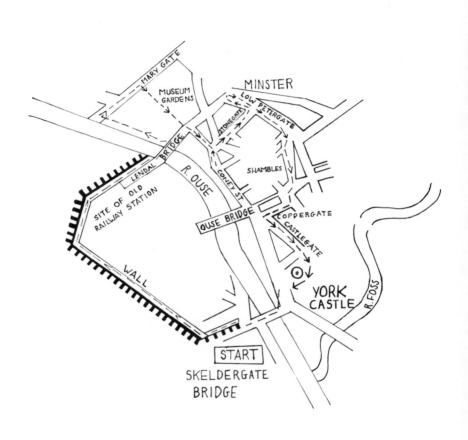

MARY GATE

MUSEUM GARDENS

MINSTER

LOW PETERGATE

STONEGATE

SHAMBLES

LENDAL BRIDGE

R. OUSE

CONEY ST.

SITE OF OLD RAILWAY STATION

OUSE BRIDGE

COPPERGATE

CASTLEGATE

WALL

YORK CASTLE

R. FOSS

START

SKELDERGATE BRIDGE

10

Expeditions to York

Although we have little direct evidence of which routes the Brontës would have taken on their various visits to York, I have chosen a route made up from what we do know and from the guide books of the time. We begin by a walk along the western half of the walls, passing below us the site of the old York railway station. We then cross the river – this would have been by ferry boat at the time – and walk along the promenade by the river and through the Museum Gardens to the site of the George Hotel where Charlotte, Anne and Ellen Nussey stayed. From here we walk as they did to the Minster and then conclude the walk by visiting the Shambles and the Castle.

Even in the time of the Brontës, York was regarded as something special. Other towns contained old buildings but few had such a concentration of late medieval houses and churches. Dickens spoke for many when he described the city as full of 'gabled houses craning their necks across the road to pry into one another's affairs ... and an infinity of shops where every commodity of life was sold'.

It is revealing of the severe constraints on the Brontës that, even though Haworth was in the York diocese until 1836, there is no evidence that any of the family had seen the city until Charlotte probably called in on her way to the coast with Ellen in September 1839.

However, it was Anne who came to know and love York through her employment at Thorp Green. It seems likely that her first visit there was because the Robinsons had someone meet her in York to take her out to Thorp Green. In any event this was to be merely the first of many visits to the old city. Mr Robinson's account book proves there were shopping expeditions to York and it seems as good as certain that Anne accompanied the family on several of these. These would have been more than shopping expeditions in our sense. York was at the very centre of fashionable life amongst the county families. Trips to York, during some of which the family stayed overnight (perhaps at the George in Coney Street), might involve attending York races, concerts, fashionable churches, parties. During these visits and the stays she would have made on the way to and from Scarborough, Anne would have got to know both the geography and the principal buildings of the old city. And it would have been her glowing descriptions of these that would have motivated the unadventurous Emily to join her in their unique excursion there within a few weeks of Anne leaving Thorp Green.

Originally they had planned to visit both York and Scarborough. Then Scarborough was dropped, probably because the cost of travel and accommodation and, most important, the sheer tedium of two extra days devoted to travelling between York and Scarborough and back – for there was still no railway line – all combined to rule out the additional journey. So it was that on Monday 30 June 1845 the two girls set out. As they must have used the coach they would have had to book in advance to secure a place inside. They would also have had to set off before dawn. For the most likely conveyance would have been the Royal Alexander from the Fleece Inn in Low Street, Keighley, the coach which may have been used by Anne to come and go from Scarborough. If it was still running at this date as it had for many years it would have left Keighley at 6.30 a.m. and the girls would have had to walk down to catch it. They would then have had to suffer the slow journey down Airedale and through Bradford to Leeds which by this date should have got them to the Rose and Crown in Leeds by a little before 10.00 a.m. There they might have been in time to catch the 9.50 train from Marsh Lane to York, which got in at 11.20. More probably they would have had to wait for the 1.10, which arrived at 2.45. You could not be in a hurry in early Victorian England!

We can only speculate in what order they would have explored the ancient city or what they would have chosen to see. They would certainly have had to walk right from the old station to the bottom of Micklegate and then turn left over Ouse Bridge and up the slight hill to Spurriergate to reach their hotel in Coney Street (Ouse Bridge was still the only bridge across the Ouse at this period). But it would not have been very long before Anne would have hauled Emily off to see York Minster. Anne's Diary Paper of 1841 lists seeing the Minster as one of the high spots of the previous five years. And we know that Anne insisted on re-visiting the Minster on her next – and last – visit to the city in 1849. It was obviously a place of pilgrimage to her.

For the rest, though, we can only guess. Guide books of the time suggest walks on the walls, that is the walls west of the river, visits to the Museum and the Museum Gardens, the Minster and other church buildings, the quaint shopping streets and the then more fearsome looking Castle with its crenellated walls. And it is hard to imagine someone so physically active as Emily not wanting to see as much of this as she could. I have, therefore, arranged my walk to follow the sort of route an early Victorian visitor might have taken.

But if we cannot be sure what the two girls saw and in what order, we can at least get some inkling of the very different ways they looked back on their trip a few weeks later. Emily first:

'Anne and I went our first long journey by ourselves together, leaving home on the 30th of June, Monday, sleeping at York, returning to Keighley Tuesday evening, sleeping there and walking home on Wednesday morning. Though the weather was broken we enjoyed ourselves very much, except during a few hours at Bradford. And during our excursion we were, Ronald Macalgin, Henry Angora, Juliet Augusteena, Rosabella Esmaldan, Ella and Julian Egremont, Catherine Navarre, and Cordelia Fitzalphnold, escaping from the palaces of instruction to join the Royalists – the Royalists who are hard driven at present by the victorious Republicans. The

York Minster from the city walls. Walks on this part of the walls were a highlight of visits to York in the time of the Brontës.

Gondals still flourish bright as ever ... We intend sticking firm by the rascals as long as they delight us, which I am glad to say they do at present.'

The visit obviously meant a great deal to Emily, who devotes far more space to it than to her stay in Brussels. What is striking is how much less the real journey and the actual city of York meant to her than the role-playing game of the Gondals which she had resumed with Anne during the trip. In all this there is a fascinating contrast with Anne. Curiously she does not mention the visit at all. And, although she says she is eager to see the Emperor Julius's *Life* which Emily is writing, she also confesses that the 'Gondals in general are not in first-rate playing condition'. Both surely point to a growing divergence between the two once close sisters. It seems possible that this very trip, meant to cement the bond between the two sisters, was the first sign they were drawing apart. If so, it is intriguing that Anne seems more aware of this than Emily.

We can just about piece together an outline of the return journey from Emily's Diary Paper, her account book and some local information. The girls returned by 'train to Leeds', the account book informs us. It seems they then took an 'omnibus' into Bradford. Here there was a hitch of some sort which led to a 'few hours in Bradford'. And the account book backs this up with a reference to a shilling paid for some wine. The best guess must be that the girls were kept waiting there for the coach to Skipton, the old Royal Alexander, which either arrived late or had to be replaced by another coach. In any case the account books refer to '2 omnibuses', which surely suggests that, however they arrived in Bradford they had to change there, the result being that they had to spend the night in Keighley and have their tea there (tea, in this context, almost certainly an evening meal). Finally next morning they walked back to Haworth.

All in all it had been quite an adventure.

THE WALK AROUND YORK

Start from Skeldergate Postern on the west side of Skeldergate Bridge. There is plenty of parking across the bridge on the east side of the river and at Nunnery Lane on the west side of the river. Climb up to the arch, go through and climb the steps on to the wall. Walk ahead passing Baile Hill on the right. Walk for about ½ mile to Micklegate Bar. Notice how the Minster rises over the rooftops as in Victorian times. At Micklegate Bar descend the steps and walk ahead through the Bar. Pause to have a look down Micklegate. Unlike so much in York the street has not altered much since the time of the Brontës. After the Bar climb back up again on to the walls. When you walk down three steps everything within the walls ahead to the right formed part of the old York Railway Station, the station by which the Brontës would have arrived and departed. Contemporary guides mention both the view of the station and the 'numerous arriving and departing trains'. The just visible arches in the walls were made to let the trains in through the walls.

As you round the corner notice the 'new' station, reputed to have been the largest railway station in the world when it was completed in 1877. When you are opposite the Royal York Hotel you can see all that is left of the original station tucked away beyond some uninspiring modern developments. The huge and impressive brick-built North Eastern Railway Headquarters was built in 1900–6. Continue over roads to the end of the walls. When you have descended the steps at the end of the wall turn left and cross Lendal Bridge. This was built in 1863–6.

At the end of Lendal Bridge turn left down some steps and turn right by Lendal Tower, formerly St Leonard's Tower. Walk away from the bridge along the Esplanade. This was constructed in 1832 and would almost certainly have been walked by the Robinsons and Anne. Paintings show this was a fashionable place to take a promenade. Walk ahead to the Water Tower and go through the arch. The space in front is where many of the boats were loaded and unloaded in the time of the Brontës. Notice the slope up to the street on the right. This was designed to ease the movement of goods.

Turn right up Marygate and walk up the street to St Olave's Church whose foundations – and dedication – date from the Anglo-Saxon period. Looking round old churches was an integral part of a visit to York in the 19th century. After looking round the church turn left and left again to enter the Museum Gardens. Like the walk on the Walls and visiting the churches, a visit to the Museum Gardens was a 'must' in Victorian times. For sixpence you were admitted both to the grounds – including the open air swimming pool which then existed at the north west corner of the Gardens – and the Museum itself. Turn left at a cross road of paths and walk through St Mary's Abbey. The Victorians were great admirers of ruins and it seems certain that Anne and her companions must at some point have walked through these.

St Mary's Abbey ruins in the museum gardens, York.

From the ruins walk right to the front of the Museum. This looked very different inside in the Victorian age with its collection of skeleta, stuffed birds etc. If you can afford the time and money it is well worth going in now, too.

With your back to the Museum entrance turn left and walk ahead out of the Museum Gardens. Cross the road and walk ahead along Lendal to St Helen's Square. Here turn right through an arch immediately to the right of the Mansion House and walk down to the Guildhall (1446), another favourite of the Victorian tourist and probably visited at some point by Anne as it is so close to where she almost certainly stayed. The inside has been totally rebuilt having been bombed in 1942. Having looked round, return to St Helen's Square and turn right. On the right you will pass St Martin le Grand, another building almost certainly visited by Anne, but also gutted in 1942. In the Brontës' time it contained some fine medieval glass. 25 yards past this church you will see an archway, a pillar and a bay window on your right. This is all that now remains of the George Hotel at which

Anne, Charlotte and Emily stayed in 1849 and Anne had probably stayed earlier. The archway was for the coaches which left this hotel for Scarborough etc.

Now retrace your steps to St Helen's Square. From now on you will be walking by the same route as Anne would have used to and from the Minster on her last visit to York and, most probably, on other occasions earlier. Turn right across St Helen's Square into Stonegate, which starts a few yards to the left of St Helen's Church. Where Stonegate meets a crossroads turn left along High Petergate. At the end of St Michael le Belfry veer right towards the entrance to the Minster. Enter York Minster and if you have sufficient energy have a good look round. Guidebooks from the time of the Brontës recommended visits to the choir, crypt, chapter house, vestry and top of the tower. In those days one of the vergers would take visitors round and ask for a tip (the vails) at each point of interest in turn. It would be surprising if Anne at least did not attend either Matins (then 10 am daily) or Evensong (then 4 pm daily).

On leaving the Minster, return round the far side of St Michael le Belfry to High Petergate. Walk straight ahead at the crossroads along Low Petergate until you come to King's Square, perhaps the greatest centre of outdoor entertainment in York today. When the Brontës visited York, a medieval church, Christ Church, the butchers' church, built, supposedly, on the site of the palace occupied by the Viking kings of York, filled the centre of the square. Veer right – but do not turn right – along the right hand pavement into the Shambles. Walk to the end of the street. Stop here and look to the left. The Old George, which some scholars have believed was the hotel at which the Brontës stayed, stood about 75 yards to your left on the site of the 1960s commercial development. Turn right towards All Saints Pavement with its unusual octagonal tower. As you approach the church fork left – but do not turn left – along Coppergate. Notice the old buildings along the right hand side. The Three Tuns has stood on that site serving beer under that name since before the time of the Brontës. Walk to the end of Coppergate and turn left into Castlegate. St Mary's Coppergate may have been another church visited by the Brontës. The guide books call it a 'fine church'. It now houses the York Story.

At the end of Castlegate walk ahead to the Castle, as it is still anachronistically called. Before this century the area was enclosed with a high battlemented wall and served as prison as well as assize courts. However, the guide books show that this too was regarded as being on the Victorian tourist itinerary. Visitors gained admission to the grounds through a castellated gatehouse at the north west corner of the area – now the car park. Walk straight ahead from the end of Castlegate to the circular lawn at the centre of the Castle. This lawn was called the Eye of Yorkshire and was at the centre of the Castle. If you have time pay a visit to the Castle Museum to your left. Otherwise turn right between the Assize Courts and Clifford's Tower. Most tourists would seem to have entered the Castle merely to view Clifford's Tower, but even in those times visitors could and did climb the walls, as the guide books show.

If by now you still have the time, money, energy and inclination, climb the steps and walls. Otherwise, with your back to Clifford's Tower, walk right to the main road ahead. Cross at the zebra crossing into the park on the other side of the road and walk half left along the path towards the river and the bridge. As you come up to the bridge turn left up some steps and then turn right along the pavement to cross the Ouse by Skeldergate Bridge. This too did not exist in the time of the Brontës. The river had to be crossed by ferry. At the far end of the bridge you will see Skeldergate Postern – and the end of your walk.

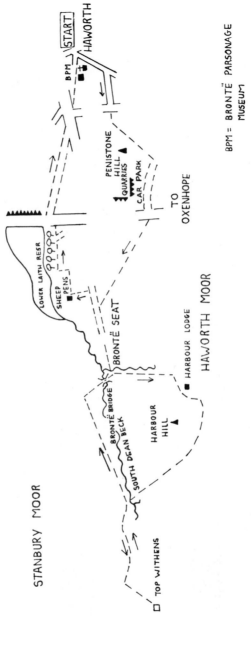

STANBURY MOOR

LOWER LAITH RESR

SHEEP PENS

BRONTË SEAT

BRONTË BRIDGE

SOUTH DEAN BECK

HARBOUR HILL

HARBOUR LODGE

HAWORTH MOOR

TOP WITHENS

START

HAWORTH

BPM

PENISTONE HILL QUARRIES

CAR PARK

TO OXENHOPE

BPM = BRONTË PARSONAGE MUSEUM

11

Haworth Moor: Emily's Inspiration for 'Wuthering Heights'

Walking Distance: 8 miles or 5 miles

This walk is centred on *Wuthering Heights*. We set out from Haworth as Emily must have so often done and walk over Penistone Hill, the obvious model for Penistone Crag, with its commanding views across the Worth valley. We then descend to join the path the girls would have used on their trips on to the moors. En route we walk below Enshaw Knoll, from whose name Emily probably derived the name of the Earnshaw family. When we reach the Brontë Bridge we follow a comparatively little used path up to Top Withens. This still gives something of the flavour of the moors before they became so popular. From Top Withens, whose site and name may have contributed to the farm Wuthering Heights, we return by the route Emily would have probably taken back to the Brontë Bridge and Haworth. When we are almost back in Haworth we detour along a route which Mr Brontë would probably have used on his pastoral visits.

Once the Brontë family moved to Haworth it was inevitable that the children would sooner or later find their way on to the moor – or Common, as it was then known. Immediately behind the Parsonage a flagged path that was the continuation of the lane up to the Parsonage crossed a field and reached a crossroads. From there the moors opened in a fan, extending south and west to Calderdale in one direction, over into Lancashire in the other.

The nearest summit was Penistone Hill. Heavily quarried at the time for its stone – including the huge rock that gave it its name – it was a place where Haworth people walked and bilberried, picked bunches of heather and let their dogs run free – an ideal place for young children to run wild. As the young motherless family explored the hill they would have seen the ravine of Sladen Beck – then without a reservoir – opening up to their right below. If they had climbed at all they would have seen Top Withens perched in its island of pastureland against the western skyline. Everywhere they would have seen those dark wastes that in summer turn so startling a violet colour. To all of them in their different ways the woods and streams would have beckoned them on to explore on and on into what was then a great silent wilderness.

Walking up on to the hills became a ritual into which only the closest of friends were initiated. Ellen Nussey was one such and has left us a vivid picture of perhaps several such explorations:

'In fine and suitable weather delightful rambles were made over the moors, and down into the glens and ravines that here and there broke the monotony of the moorland. The rugged bank and rippling brook were treasures of delight. Emily, Anne and Branwell used to ford the streams, and sometimes placed stepping stones for the other two; there was always a lingering delight in these spots – every moss, every flower, every tint and form were noted and enjoyed. Emily especially had a gleesome delight in these nooks of beauty – her reserve for a time vanished. One long ramble made in these early days was far away over the moors to a spot familiar to Emily and Anne which they called 'The Meeting of the Waters'. It was a small oasis of emerald green turf, broken here and there by small clear springs; a few large stones served as resting places; seated here we were hidden from all the world, nothing appearing in view but miles and miles of heather, a glorious blue sky, and brightening sun. A fresh breeze wafted on us its exhilarating influence; we laughed and made mirth of each other, and settled we could call ourselves the quartette. Emily, half reclining on a slab of stone, played like a

Haworth Parsonage, where the Brontë children lived and produced their greatest work.

young child with the tadpoles in the water, making them swim about.'

The clear implication of this is that the moors meant more to the other children than they did to Charlotte. It is noticeable that it was the three children younger than her that would first ford the streams and then pile up stones for Charlotte and Emily to cross. Daphne Du Maurier tells us that Branwell and Emily would often go on long expeditions together, ranging as far away as Heptonstall and Wycoller. And certainly Francis Grundy, who met Branwell when he was employed in Calderdale, tells us that Branwell still loved to escape to the moors.

Though Branwell loved the moors, they are principally — and rightly — associated with Emily. Constrained in company she was most herself when out on the hills. An early biographer who had access to many local people who remembered Emily, A. Mary F. Robinson, tells us: 'In 1833 Emily was nearly fifteen, a tall long-armed girl, full grown, elastic of tread; with a slight figure that looked queenly in her best dresses, but loose and boyish when she slouched over the moors, whistling to her dogs, and taking long strides over the rough earth.' And Miss Robinson later adds the following charming anecdote: 'Out of doors, Emily made friends with all the beasts and birds. She would come home carrying in her hands some young bird or rabbit, and softly talking to it as she came. "Ee, Miss Emily," the young servant would say, "one would think the bird could understand you." "I am sure it can," Emily would answer. "Oh, I am sure it can."' Another author who also met people who knew the Brontës well, Halliwell Sutcliffe, describes (or imagines?) her sitting by the fire at Top Withens: 'We follow this shrinking girl, who scarce dares pass the time of day with her equals, and find her sitting at her ease on the kitchen long-settle, with the shining pewter behind her on the walls and overhead the oatcake hanging from the creel. She has lost her shyness with the first step across the threshold; she talks like the upland folk who have given her welcome, slowly and with surety, and into her speech there steals many a pithy proverb, many a touch of that graphic simile which is part and parcel of the upland tongue. Presently she will go to the far mistal, to have a look at the roan cow or to see how it is faring with the wye calves, newly weaned.'

There were two aspects to this love of the wild. Notoriously, she always pined when she was away from home. So Ellen Nussey in a letter to Mrs Gaskell says of her stay at Roe Head: 'Emily Brontë went to Roe Head as pupil when Charlotte went as teacher; she stayed there two months; she never settled, and was ill from nothing more than homesickness.' Charlotte tells us with more circumstantial detail: 'Every morning when she woke the vision of home and the moors rushed on her, and darkened and saddened the day before her ... I felt in my heart she would die, if she did not go home, and with this conviction obtained her recall.'

But the greatest proof of Emily's love of the moors was of course in her novel, *Wuthering Heights*. For, although the topography of the novel is different from that of the Worth valley – and even more unlike that of the Shibden valley, with which some people equate it – there can be no doubt that the Haworth moors were in Emily's mind as she re-arranged hills and dales, rivers and settlements to create the scenery of her novel. Thus when she was looking for a name to encompass the whole range of hills on which her farm was situated, she chose the name Wuthering Heights with its obvious echo of the name Withens Height, the hill above Top Withens (where Ellen suggested the novel was set). More explicitly still she named the topmost peak of her range Penistone Crag – with its obvious echo of the local Penistone Hill. Even the name of the principal family seems deliberately selected to sound local: Earnshaw is the closest she could get by way of a surname to Enshaw, the name of the knoll roughly midway between Withens Height and Penistone Hill. The ecology of the novel is much closer to that of the Worth moors than anywhere else, for though there are plenty of moors and crags, weatherbeaten farms and secluded manor houses in the

The lane from the parsonage to Haworth church.

southern Pennines, heather and grouse are found more plenti-
fully round Haworth than many areas – certainly than round
the Shibden valley.

The whole book in fact is centred on the tug of war
between the world of the moors and the temptations offered
by the lowlands. It is no accident that the ancient stone-built
house, Wuthering Heights, has the same name as the range
on which it stands – nor that the family who inhabit it have
names connected with the wilderness in which they grow up,
marry and die – to vanish back into the earth again. Thus
'Earnshaw' means 'the wood of the eagles'; 'Hindley', 'the
field of the hinds'; and 'Hareton', 'the town of the hare'; all
allude to some of the wild creatures that at different times
have inhabited these uplands; 'Heathcliff', a name originally
given to 'a son who had died in childhood' speaks for itself.
At various points he is actually described in terms more
suggestive of wild nature than a human being. 'Tell her what
Heathcliff is', Catherine is made to say at one point, 'An
unreclaimed creature without refinement, without cultiva-
tion: an arid wilderness of furze and whinstone.'

Charlotte, as always, got it right when in her preface to the
'New Edition' she wrote: '*Wuthering Heights* was hewn in a
wild workshop, with simple tools, out of homely materials.
The statuary found a granite block on a solitary moor; gazing
thereon, he saw how from the crag might be elicited a head,
savage, swart, sinister; a form moulded with at least one
element of grandeur – power. He wrought with a rude chisel,
and from no model but the vision of his meditations. With
time and labour, the crag took human shape; and there it
stands colossal, dark and frowning, half statue, half rock: in
the former sense, terrible and goblin-like; in the latter, almost
beautiful, for its colouring is of mellow grey, and moorland
moss clothes it; and heath, with its blooming bells and balmy
fragrance, grows faithfully close to the giant's foot.'

THE WALK OVER HAWORTH MOOR

The walk starts at the top of Haworth. There is a bus service from Keighley and ample parking for cars – provided that you do not arrive after noon on a Saturday or Sunday in summer or a bank holiday. Start from the bottom of the church steps by the Black Bull at the top of the main street. Walk up the steps and through the gate into the churchyard. Turn left before the church and walk ahead along the flagged path between the iron railings – not turning right – to a kissing gate. Through this, walk ahead along the flagged path. You are now on the Brontë Way, which you will follow for the next mile and a half, and also on the route by which Charlotte used to walk to meet her fiancé, Arthur Bell Nicholls. Where there is a sort of crossroads of paths turn right along the route posted 'Brontë Way, Brontë Falls, Top Withens' (and some words in Japanese) along a rough farm track. Walk up to the metalled road ahead.

Across the road you will see Penistone Hill. The name of the hill and some of its details must have been in Emily's mind when she called the summit above the farm, Wuthering Heights, Penistone Crags. Cross the road and take the left fork – again marked by the same signs. At a crossroads of paths again fork left and climb uphill. At the top of the rise fork right to the OS trig point at the summit of the hill. From here on a good day you can see not only the hills surrounding the Worth Valley, Nab Hill, Oxenhope Stoop Hill, Withens Height, Crow Hill, but also, further away, Pendle Hill – 'old Pendle' in a letter of Charlotte's to Lady Kay-Shuttleworth – and the Craven Pennines beyond Skipton. Unless you fancy an adventure in the old quarries ahead go back down to the footpath from which you came and turn right.

Now follow the main path – once or twice posted – first to a wooden pavilion and then around the left hand edge of an old quarry to an extensive gravel car park. From the car park follow the gravel road ahead. When it forks take the right branch. When you come after about 60 yards to a crossroads of paths walk straight ahead. When you come to the main road, walk straight across and follow a much smaller foot-path to a kissing gate. Go through the gate and follow the path as it veers half right across the moor. You will pass a huge sign – not in Japanese – which indicates the way. The pleasant, mostly dry path contours across the side of the moor to join a large track to the left of a stone wall. Follow this large track along the left hand side of the wall and then straight ahead when the wall veers off to the right. You will gradually lose height, sometimes down stone steps, until you finally come down to a meeting of two small streams where you will see a stone shaped like a seat (the Brontë Seat), a flagged bridge (the Brontë Bridge) and a tiny waterfall (the Brontë Waterfall). At this point you can either walk ahead to Top Withens, which will add another 3 miles to the walk (**see Section A**), or return to Haworth by a different route (**see Section B**).

A. At this point the Withens sign points across the flagged bridge. For a quieter, more atmospheric route, turn left up the narrow path to the right of the Brontë Waterfall. Zigzag uphill. The best view of the 'falls' is to be had about half way up the path. When level with the top of the falls do not cross the stream but zigzag uphill to the right by a narrow path about 10 yards beyond the falls. Where you meet another larger path turn left and follow it as it keeps to the right of the stream towards a large stone house behind a wall amongst some trees. There is no evidence that Emily was thinking of this house as the exemplar for her Wuthering Heights, but the position of the house below a hill and with its field sur-rounded by moorland is probably as close as we can now come to seeing how the surroundings of Wuthering Heights may have looked, though the house itself, of course, does not have even the remotest resemblance to the one in the novel. When you reach a signpost a few yards from a wooden footbridge turn right to follow the right hand side of a stone wall uphill.

Penistone Hill, the obvious model for the Penistone Crag of Wuthering Heights.

This path is never as clear as the ones on which you have been walking until now. However, if you keep approximately 10 yards to the right of the wall you will see increasing signs of it. When the wall bends left, curve slightly to the left and then wind round right into a shallow valley. In August and early September when the heather is out the scene is quite unbelievable. As you reach the col at the head of the shallow valley you will see Top Withens ahead across the moor. Do not take the ancient trackway uphill to the left but keep straight ahead on another less clear path to the right of some marshy ground and then a stream. There are marvellous views ahead to Simon's Seat, Great Whernside and Beamsley Beacon. Keep the stream on your left and below you and walk downhill for about 300 yards. At a point where two streams meet, cross over as best you can to a clear path on the far side of both streams and follow it as it curves uphill to meet another larger path. Turn left and follow this towards the ruin on the skyline, Top Withens. From here on the route barely requires description. One is tempted to say, as Wain-wright does in one of his guides, that if you lose your way here you should seriously consider giving up hillwalking.

However, as the weather is not always as clement as it should be I include some notes. Follow the path as it gently contours downhill to yet another meeting of streams. Cross over – again as best you can – to a path between the two streams and climb a clear path uphill through a ruined wall to meet another path, the Pennine Way, at a sort of T-junction of paths with a signpost. Turn left and in a few more yards you will arrive at Top Withens, the most popular choice for the site of Wuthering Heights since Ellen Nussey identified it as such. Stay for a while and savour the atmosphere.

When you have had your fill, return to the signpost and turn right down the path marked 'Haworth' and 'Brontë Falls'. Walk back downhill by the way you came to the place where the two streams meet. Cross over and follow the path as it contours its way above Sladen Beck. Do not turn right for Harbour Lodge. Walk ahead for ⅓ mile. When a wall comes up from the valley keep to its left hand side for 30 yards, then cross by a ladder stile. Walk ahead to another wall. Again keep to the left hand side and walk ahead by a stone stoop (post) to a wooden gate. Go through and walk along the right hand side of the wall. Once through the next stile walk across a field filled with rushes and then start sloping your way downhill. There are good views of the area round the Brontë Waterfall. As you continue downhill you will see a gate. Go through this and the stone gateway down to the bridge and Brontë Seat.

B. With your back to the Brontë Seat walk uphill and follow the excellent path as it winds, climbs and contours its way along the right hand side of Sladen Beck back towards Haworth. When the wall comes up from the left continue alongside. After about ¾ mile you will see a double gate on your left with a notice alongside saying 'Dogs Must Be Kept On A Lead'. Climb over this gate and walk downhill to the

The Sunday School where Charlotte taught in Haworth.

barn ahead. Enter the labyrinthine sheep-pens (which should provide some entertainment to any children in the party) and turn right to a small gate which provides an exit into the field. Walk ahead to a gate and once through it follow a wall to some ruined buildings. Descend into a dip and on the far side look for some steps leading up to an intimidating looking stile (which is by no means as hard as it looks).

Once through this stile turn half left to the corner of the field by a wood. Go through the stile and walk along the edge of the wood to a gate. Through this go along a short length of enclosed path to another gate. Still keeping to the right hand side of the wood walk to another gate. Through this you are on the ancient road from Oxenhope to Stanbury. Turn right uphill for 30 yards. Pass a field gate on your left and go through a rusty iron gate into a field. Walk ahead to a gate between a timber building and farmhouse. Go through this and walk ahead to a stile. This is by far the worst on the whole walk. Once again children should find it fun.

Take care as you enter the road – the modern road from

Oxenhope to Stanbury – and turn left down the left hand pavement until you reach the bottom of the hill. Here cross over to another road signposted for Haworth. The first few yards are not exactly the best scenery on the walk but as you climb uphill you will command a fine view across the Worth Valley. When you join another road coming in from the right walk ahead. It is sometimes busy, but there is a pleasant footpath along the left hand side. Do not turn either to right or left at a sort of staggered crossroads. Walk ahead with a small wood to your right until you see a stile on your right. Go through this and follow the flagged path across the fields and by some houses until you reach the Brontë Parsonage Museum and the centre of Haworth, where the walk began.

12

Scarborough:
Anne's Last Resting Place

Walking Distance: 3 miles

This route is based very closely on places known to have been visited by Anne. We begin from St Nicholas Cliff where she — and later other members of the family — stayed. We cross the Spa footbridge and walk through the Spa grounds down to the Spa itself. We then descend to the sands to pass the site of the bathing huts used by people staying on the Cliff in the early 19th century. We now cross the sands as Anne did in her donkey cart on her last visit to the resort to pay a brief visit to the picturesque old fishing town. After this we climb up to the Castle, the scene of the proposal in *Agnes Grey*. Finally we return by the churchyard in which Anne is buried and through some of the streets which were at the heart of fashionable Scarborough at the time.

Scarborough played its part in the Brontë story and literary achievement. In the 1840s it was at the very pinnacle of its fashionable heyday. 'The Queen of Sea-Bathing Places', 'a picturesque place perched on lofty cliffs', 'a bay of Naples on the north east coast of England' are just a few of the eulogies one can find in guides to the spas of England. Up on the Cliff, as it was called, the part of the town in which Charlotte, Ellen and Anne stayed, the nobility and upper middle classes would rent rooms knowing that all around them they would find people of the same background as themselves. For not only were there the waters to be 'taken', there were concerts at the Spa and just around the corner the Theatre Royal on St Thomas Street. In addition there were horse-races across the sands, dances, private parties, a fashionable church to attend and, of course, promenades across the bridge and along the

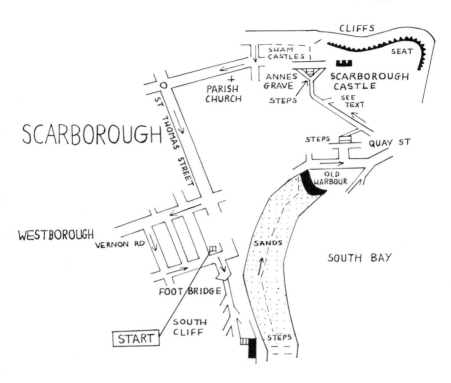

South Cliff. For a few weeks in the summer Scarborough was at the fashionable heart of the North of England.

The first of the Brontës to visit Scarborough was Anne who came to the resort every summer in the company of the Robinson family while she worked for them – that is in 1841, 1842, 1843, 1844 and possibly 1840. New arrivals were noted in the local papers, the *Scarborough Gazette* and the *Scarborough Herald*, which would also record where the visitors were staying. In the case of the Robinsons this was Wood's Lodgings on St Nicholas Cliff, amongst the most prestigious lodging houses in the resort. Long demolished, it stood in the same commanding position as the present Grand Hotel. However, there are enough surviving pictures of it to be able to construct a picture of what kind of building it was. As seen from St Nicholas Cliff it was a pleasantly plain three-storey Georgian domestic building which faced down on to a quiet and fashionable street and the gardens that it contained. As seen, however, from the sands, it was altogether more impressive – a sort of Regency palazzo with pilasters and balustrades. It looked in fact what it was – a building designed for the privileged. Contemporary advertisements spoke of 'an uninterrupted view of the sea', but there was far more to it than that. The rooms were as spacious and modern as in many a wealthy town house and no doubt comparably furnished. Grassy lawns sloped down from the premises on one side to the bathing huts lining the edge of the sands, on the other to the fashionable Rotunda Museum. Nor was it any worse on the town side. Most amenities were no more than a few steps away. One really was at the heart of things. Just to be seen entering and leaving Wood's Lodgings said more about one's social standing than any number of words.

However, the most revealing thing that Anne tells us about Scarborough under its thin disguise of 'A ____' in *Agnes Grey* is the way that it represents the antithesis of the ugly class-snobbery which gives so much of its sharp focus to the story. Perhaps this reflected real life. Certainly it was to remain an enchanted place for her. The description in Chapter 24 of *Agnes Grey* may offer us a picture of how she managed to take her modest pleasures amidst all the routine:

'I would often gladly pierce the town to obtain the pleasure of a walk beside it (sc. the sea) whether with the pupils or alone with my mother during the vacations. It was delightful to me at all time and seasons.'

The description of the morning when the heroine got up early in order to saunter alone on the sands seems as near to reminiscence as we find anywhere in Anne:

'I was dressed and out, when the church clock struck a quarter to six. There was a feeling of freshness and vigour on the very streets, and when I got free of the town, when my foot was on the sands and my face towards the broad, bright

A contemporary engraving of Scarborough as Anne knew it. To the right is the building she occupied during her last illness. The Grand Hotel now stands there.

bay, no language can describe the effect of the deep clear azure of the sky and ocean, the bright morning sunshine on the semi-circular barrier of craggy cliffs surmounted by green swelling hills and on the smooth, wide sands, and the low rocks out at sea looking, with their clothing of weed and moss, like little grass grown islands and above all, on brilliant, sparkling waves.'

There is nothing so explicit or climactic in *The Tenant of Wildfell Hall*, but even in this novel Anne had not forgotten the Yorkshire coast. The landscape and ecology in the book are very similar to those of the North York Moors somewhere to the north of Scarborough as Chapters 5 and 6 of the novel show. Thus it is four miles from the hall to the sea, but there are some hills between which stop one seeing it until it suddenly bursts into view below as one gains the top of a cliff. The terrain around the hall mostly consists of wooded valleys with hills between, some of which have cornfields on top. However, the highest points of the hills are either bare grass sheep-pastures or heather and bilberry-covered moorland – precisely the sort of country Anne would have seen had she ventured inland from Scarborough. Indeed the geography of the book as a whole seems to centre on the contrasts Anne would have experienced during the early 1840s. On the one hand one has the lowland *Grass*dale – perhaps Thorp *Green*; on the other hand Wild*fell* Hall, the North York *Moors*. The sea-scapes within this framework are both important in themselves but also, as in *Agnes Grey*, as something that brings out the deep affinity between the hero and the heroine. In Anne's fiction the sea does the job that the moors do in Emily's.

In view of this deep significance of the sea to Anne it is not surprising that it was Anne's last wish that she should have the chance to see the sea once more. And despite misgivings this is what Charlotte decided to give her. The two sisters decided they would go to Scarborough to some accommodation on Anne's beloved St Nicholas Cliff and Ellen Nussey agreed to accompany them.

The accommodation they took was a 'good sized sitting room and an airy double-bedded room (both commanding a good sea view)' – at a Mrs Jefferson's at No 2 The Cliff. This accommodation – now also swallowed up in the Grand Hotel – was almost next door to Wood's Lodgings, but a good deal cheaper. The only surviving photograph of the accommodation in Scarborough Library suggests it dated from before Scarborough's development as a fashionable resort. It was probably the middle one in a row of perhaps three modest two-floor cottages facing west. It was as close as Charlotte could arrange – or afford? – to the accommodation in which Anne had seemingly been so happy. However, I shall leave the rest to Ellen:

'On the 25th we arrived at Scarborough; our dear invalid having, during the journey, directed our attention to every prospect worthy of note.

'On the 26th she drove on the sands for an hour; and lest the poor donkey should be urged by its driver to a greater

Scarborough castle ruins. Although the castle is not mentioned, Anne seems to have had this location in mind for the conclusion of her Agnes Grey.

speed than her tender heart thought right, she took the reins, and drove herself. When joined by her friend, she was charging the boy-master of the donkey to treat the poor animal well. She was ever fond of dumb things and would give up her own comfort for them.

'On Sunday, the 27th, she wished to go to church, and her eye brightened with the thought of once more worshipping her God amongst her fellow-creatures. We thought it prudent to dissuade her from the attempt, though it was evident her heart was longing to join in the public act of devotion and praise.

'She walked a little in the afternoon, and meeting with a sheltered and comfortable seat near the beach, she begged we would leave her, and enjoy the various scenes near at hand, which were new to us, but familiar to her. She loved the place, and wished us to share her preference.

'The evening closed in with the most glorious sunset ever witnessed. The castle on the cliff stood in proud glory gilded by the rays of the declining sun. The distant ships glittered like burnished gold; the little boats near the beach heaved on the ebbing tide, inviting occupants. The view was grand beyond description. Anne was drawn in her easy chair to the window, to enjoy the scene with us. Her face became illumined almost as much as the glorious scene she gazed upon. Little was said, for it was plain that her thoughts were driven by the imposing view before her to penetrate forwards to the regions of unfading glory. She again thought of public worship, and wished us to leave her, and join those who were assembled at the House of God. We declined gently urging the duty and pleasure of staying with her, who was now so dear and so feeble. On returning to her place near the fire, she conversed with her sister upon the propriety of returning to their home. She did not wish it for her own sake, she said; she was fearing others might suffer more if her decease occurred where she was. She probably thought the task of accompanying her lifeless remains on a long journey was more than her sister could bear – more than the bereaved father could bear, were she borne home another, and a third tenant of the family-vault in the short space of nine months.

'The night was passed without any apparent accession of illness. She rose at seven o'clock, and performed most of her toilet herself, by her expressed wish. Her sister always yielded such points, believing it was the truest kindness not to press inability when it was not acknowledged. Nothing occurred to excite alarm till about 11 am. She then spoke of feeling a change. "She believed she had not long to live. Could she reach home alive, if we prepared immediately for departure?" A physician was sent for, her address to him was made with perfect composure. She begged him to say "How long he thought she might live; – not to fear speaking the truth, for she was not afraid to die." The doctor reluctantly admitted that the angel of death was already arrived, and that life was ebbing fast. She thanked him for his truthfulness, and he departed to come again very soon. She still occupied her easy chair, looking so serene, so reliant: there was no opening for grief as yet, though all knew the separation was at hand. She clasped her hands, and reverently invoked a blessing from on high; first upon her sister, then upon her friend, to whom she said, "be a sister in my stead. Give Charlotte as much of your company as you can." She then thanked each for her kindness and attention.

'Ere long the restlessness of approaching death appeared, and she was borne to the sofa; on being asked if she were easier, she looked gratefully at her questioner and said, "It is not *you* who can give me ease, but soon all will be well, through the merits of our Redeemer." Shortly after this, seeing that her sister could hardly restrain her grief, she said, "Take courage, Charlotte; take courage." Her faith never failed, and her eye never dimmed till about two o'clock, when she calmly, and without a sign, passed from the temporal to the eternal.'

THE WALK AROUND SCARBOROUGH

The walk begins from the Tourist Information Office at the corner of Huntriss Row and Falconers Road. With your back to the Tourist Office walk ahead into the street called St Nicholas Cliff. In spite of the pleasant Victorian layout of the street it has altered a great deal since the Robinsons and Branwell and Anne stayed at Wood's Lodgings. In their day there was an attractive circular formal garden in the middle of the street encircled with iron railings. And the pleasant late Georgian house in which they stayed has been replaced by the Grand Hotel. However, the view across the South Bay was the same and the street was the most prestigious place to stay in the town. Walk down the Cliff towards the bridge ahead, noting the plaque commemorating Anne Brontë on the Grand Hotel.

At the end of St Nicholas Cliff walk down on to the Spa Footbridge. This was opened on 19 July 1827. In Anne's time there was a tollbooth and gateway at the start of the bridge and a toll had to be paid to cross. A monthly ticket cost 2/6. Cross on to the bridge. This was much narrower in Victorian

Anne's grave at Scarborough.

times. It was both a fashionable place to promenade and also to watch the horse racing that then took place on the sands below. If you walk a few yards further and stop to look down to the right you will see the fine Classical-style Rotunda Museum below. This too was a great attraction in Victorian times and it is explicitly mentioned in Branwell's unfinished novel *And the Weary are at Rest*. Cross to the end of the bridge and on to the South Cliff. When the path forks, take the left hand fork. At a second fork keep right and then at a third fork by a pleasant wooden shelter take another left fork. Turn left down the first set of steps and then turn right for the Spa.

Impressive as it is, this building is later than the Brontës. In their time the Spa was a castellated structure not unlike the 'mock castles' close to Scarborough Castle. In those times it was the focal point of social life at the resort. Not merely did people go there to take the waters; the musical life of Scarborough centred on the Spa. (If you wish to explore the present building (opened 1880) walk along the left hand side to the end and return.)

Whether or not you have looked round the outside of the Spa building descend the steps at the north end. These seem to have existed even in the time of the Brontës. Turn left along the colonnade and at its end cross the road and go down some stone steps on to the sand. It seems likely that like Agnes Grey in Chapter 24 of the novel Anne too must have come down here in the early morning and savoured the still attractive solitude.

Now walk in the general direction of the Castle. When the Robinsons and Anne visited Scarborough there was no promenade. A grassy and wooded slope swept down from St Nicholas Cliff to the sands and along the edge of the sands there was a line of bathing huts, some of which could be towed down to the sea. What made Scarborough special as a spa was the fact that it combined these facilities with its mineral waters. And it seems more than likely that both the Robinsons and Anne would have taken advantage of the sea-bathing.

As you approach that part of the town below the Castle, the ancient heart of Scarborough, aim for the left hand end of the harbour wall. Note the donkeys as you approach it. It seems almost certain that Anne's last ride in a donkey cart two days before she died took place between St Nicholas Cliff and here. As you approach the harbour wall it is probably easiest to walk to the right of the Lifeboat Station and climb up the ramp to the road. The sand to the left tends to be softer and to find its way into one's shoes. Once by the road turn right and walk along the right hand pavement of Sandside keeping the Old Harbour to your right. The piers were built in 1732, 1790 and 1817, so the harbour had assumed its present form by the time the Brontës visited Scarborough and was the centre of and the chief source of employment to the old fishing town on the hillside above.

As you walk along notice King Richard III's house on the opposite side of the road. Richard III is supposed to have stayed there in 1483 but the stone casing of the house is later – probably Tudor. When you are almost at the end of the Old

The old fishing port of Scarborough. This scene cannot have altered a great deal since the Brontës' time.

Harbour — about 50 yards short of the Funfair — cross the road to Ivy House and Quay Street. If you have time, note the old buildings on Quay Street surviving from Scarborough's fishing past. In any event climb Salmon Steps, turn right for 20 yards and then turn very sharp left up some stone steps and a gradually sloping path. You now have various options.

A. If it is before 4 pm and you would like to walk up to the Castle by a more adventurous route, turn very sharp right up a stepped gravel path posted 'Sally Port Entrance'. Zigzag your way up this path until you come to a stone wall. Turn right behind this wall and climb up some stone steps to a gate into the Castle. (If this gate is closed go back down to the wall and turn right. Eventually the path levels out and you command an outstanding view of the South Bay. When the path forks take the left hand fork and, when you reach the arch, climb the steps up to the left and then turn right into the Castle.)

B. If you would like to reach the Castle by a more sedate route, ignore the gravel path off to the right signposted 'Sally Port Entrance' and proceed ahead uphill along the broad tarmacked path. After about 300 yards you will see the moat of the Castle to your right. Fifty or so yards later the path divides. Do not take either the left branch or the right but climb the steps between them. At the top of the steps turn right into Scarborough Castle.

The Castle too has altered since Anne explored it. Then there was a barracks and contemporary pictures show soldiers at the approach to the Barbican standing on guard with their rifles. Now there is nothing more disconcerting than English Heritage. It is worth exploring the Castle in some detail and, when you have done so, walking to the far end of the Castle grounds to a seat at their north east corner. For my money, this is the finest view on the whole of the Yorkshire coast. Inland you can see the hills and forests beyond Hackness; to the north, one cliff after another along the Cleveland coast; to the south, Filey Brigg and Flamborough Head.

After you have left the Castle walk down the road for about 10 yards then turn right up some steps and along a path to the right of a Gothic mansion. The old spa building bore some affinities to this and other sham castles here. Keep left when a path comes up to join you from the right. And do the same again when two more come from the right within two or three yards of each other. Almost immediately after, turn left through some large stone bollards and walk down by the 'Castle by the Sea Hotel' to the crossroads ahead. Across the road to the left you will see an extension to the churchyard. Cross into this by a gateway and turn to the left. Twenty yards ahead you will see Anne Brontë's grave.

When you have left the graveyard walk ahead along the road keeping St Mary's Church to your left. Anne Brontë seems to have had this area in mind when in Chapter 25 of *Agnes Grey* she describes how Agnes and Mr Weston climb by 'the venerable old church and the ... hill with the deep blue sea beyond it' to reach the point at which they see the sunset and he makes his proposal. As you continue down Castle Road you will pass through accommodation which still has something of the flavour of early Victorian Scarborough and pass by Wilson's Mariners' Asylum of 1836. (Contemporary guidebooks recommended seeing these.) Do not turn left until you reach the roundabout. Then turn left down St Thomas Street (Tanner Street in the time of the Brontës). There are still two theatres on the street, but the theatre in which Henry Roxby, who eloped with Lydia Robinson, acted – the theatre, that is, which Anne and the Robinsons would have visited – was on the left hand side of the street on the site of the present day night club. When you reach the end of the street the largest circulating library in the town, one surely used by both Anne and Branwell, was housed in a building on the right hand corner.

At the end of St Thomas Street turn right up the pedestrianised Newborough. Pass by two streets off to the left and turn down the third, Vernon Road. The church which the Robinsons attended and at which Anne's funeral service was held was a few yards into the street on the left. It was an attractive church with lancet windows and a fine tower which appears in many old pictures of Scarborough. Like much else in this part of the town it has been replaced by buildings of the utmost banality. The dismal building on the left, Christ Church House, stands like a tombstone in place of the vanished church. Walk past the fine Library. In the 1840s this was the Oddfellows' Hall. Interestingly, Mr Robinson's last recorded payment of money was to the Oddfellows and about 60 Oddfellows followed behind the family at his funeral according to a local diarist, George Whitehead of Ouseburn. At the end of Vernon Road turn left into Falconers Road. In a few yards you will be back at the Tourist Information Centre.

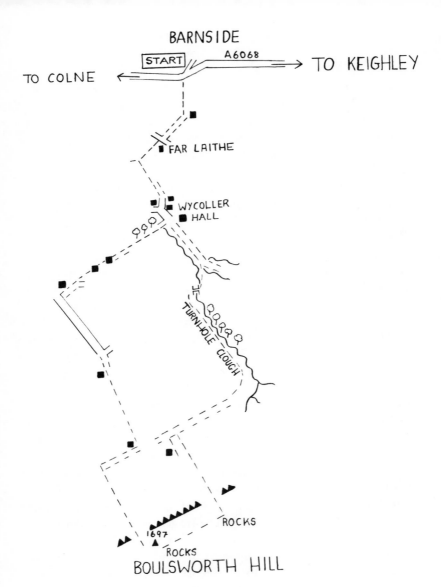

13

Wycoller Hall: The Ferndean Manor of 'Jane Eyre'?

Walking Distance: 10 miles

We begin from Barnside from which the Brontë girls were once seen walking over to Wycoller. We walk across the fields to Wycoller Hall, a possible original for Ferndean Manor in *Jane Eyre* and some of whose features may also have been used in *Wuthering Heights*. From here we follow the route the Brontës would have used to go over to Haworth – now part of the Brontë Way – but branch off to climb Boulsworth Hill. This is the highest summit in the Brontë Country and commands an outstanding view of the South Pennines. We then return by a different route across the fields to Wycoller and Barnside.

Wycoller has traditionally been associated with the Brontës. Indeed the new Brontë Way, a new long distance footpath, passes by Wycoller on its way from Gawthorpe near Padiham to Oakwell Hall. But beyond the supposed link between Wycoller Hall and Ferndean Manor, the proximity to Haworth and some attractive scenery it is not immediately obvious why Wycoller should have this privileged status as opposed to numerous other valleys and villages in the area, the Hebden valleys, for example.

However, there is perhaps more to be said for Wycoller than meets the eye. It is interesting that in Mrs Gaskell's *Life* she quotes the following story about an earlier squire of Wycoller Hall to show how wild life was in the Haworth area.

'Another squire of more distinguished family and larger

property – one is thence led to imagine of better education, but that does·not always follow – died at his house not many miles from Haworth, only a few years ago – his great amusement and occupation had been cockfighting. When he was confined to his chamber with what he knew would be his last illness, he had his cocks brought up there and watched the bloody battle from his bed. As his mortal disease increased, and it became impossible for him to turn so as to follow the combat he had looking glasses arranged in such a manner, around and above him, as he lay, that he could see the cocks fighting. And in this manner he died.'

The general consensus is that the story relates to Henry Owen Cunliffe. He had been born Henry Owen in Sheffield in 1752, but had been made heir by Henry Cunliffe on condition that he took the name Cunliffe. Henry Owen Cunliffe took over the hall in June 1773, soon after married into a wealthy family and immediately threw himself into raising the social profile of the Cunliffe family. It was he who gave the hall the appearance the Brontës would have known: he had the medieval-style fireplace installed in the great hall, inserted mullioned windows along the west wall and added an impressive porch with ornate finials. He converted, in fact, what was little more than a large yeoman's house into a fitting seat for a proud member of the local gentry. It was a startlingly early example of mock-Jacobean.

After his death, because of his extravagance, the property he left was mortgaged up to the hilt. So over the next 50 years or so, the period, that is, that the Brontës would have known it, the heirs disposed of one farm after another. The mortgagee, Henry Owen Cunliffe's wife's cousin, the Rev J Oldham, had the fine timber round the house felled and allowed the house itself to fall into progressive disrepair. By the time Edward Baines wrote his *History of Lancashire* he could describe the house as 'in ruins'.

So what evidence is there that the Brontës knew the house and the village? The first piece of evidence appears in Charlotte's juvenilia. Although she never mentions Wycoller by

Wycoller Hall today, a possible original for the 'Ferndean Manor' of Jane Eyre.

name, she does allude to other places in the vicinity: Boulsworth Hill which looms up above the head of Wycoller Dene and Colne Moss, the flat swampy ground at the top of the pass between Colne and Keighley. There are some vividly written lines which capture something of the atmosphere of the dusk there:

> 'And from the crags of Pendlebrow
>   the russet grab is gone
> And Boulsworth off his giant sides rolls
>   down the vapours dim.'

There is also some local evidence that some of the people in the vicinity recognised and remembered the Brontës. *The Lancashire and Cheshire Antiquarian Society Transactions* Vol 19 (1901) p 251 recorded that some visiting ladies 'were pleased to hear that some old folks had been spoken to who had remembered the Misses Brontë coming down from Barn-

side'. They also asserted that Wycoller Hall was the original
Fern Dene and that the hills above the valley were Wuthering
Heights. In all this, the mention of Barnside, the area to the
north of the Colne to Keighley road east of Laneshaw Bridge,
is especially striking. If the story were legend one would have
expected a far more plausible direction to have been mentioned. And that this is genuine recollection seems confirmed
by another passage from Charlotte's juvenilia, the reference
to a view from a window on Colne Moss: 'When she looked
out on the dusky sky – between the curtains of her bay-
window – fancy seemed to trace on the horizon the bare
outline of the moors – just as seen from the parlour at Colne
Moss – the evening star hung over the brow of Boulshill – the
farm fields stretched away between.' This is so accurate in its
picture of the view from Barnside, and so circumstantial in its
place-names, it surely compels us to accept that Charlotte
really had been, in circumstances for ever unknown, in the
vicinity of Barnside and, if the witness is correct, had been
accompanied by one or more of her sisters, years before her
stint at Stone Gappe. And if this is so we are perhaps justified
in looking for Wycoller influence on the novels.

For by the Brontës' time Wycoller Hall had developed a
quite fearsome reputation. As early as 1779 a local diary tells
us a room in the house was regarded as haunted, the supposed ghost being of a wife of one of the Cunliffes who had
been murdered there years before. More strikingly still, in his
Annals of Trawden Forest, the local historian Fred Bannister
tells us that the girl was of West Indian origin and that
Cunliffe had thrown her overboard on the way home. One's
suspicion that the story was influenced by *Jane Eyre* is surely
allayed by the differences between his account and both
Charlotte's story and other local versions. If any of this is true
it strongly suggests Charlotte listened to and combined
Wycoller legends obviously with others too at some points –
the more Gothic points – in *Jane Eyre*. This would include
the remote, deserted hall, the West Indian wife, the sinister
room in the house, possibly the name Eyre and last but not

least the fund of local stories about mysterious horsemen and the gytrash – interestingly linked together in *Jane Eyre*.

Charlotte describes her Ferndean Manor in the last chapter of *Jane Eyre*: 'The manor house of Ferndean was a building of considerable antiquity, moderate size and no architectural pretensions, deep buried in a wood ... His father had purchased the estate for the sake of the game covers. He would have let the house; but could find no tenant, in consequence of its ineligible and unsalubrious site. Ferndean then remained uninhabited and unfurnished; with the exception of some two or three rooms fitted up for the accommodation of the squire when he went there in the season to shoot.' There is little here specifically to identify Wycoller Hall. And when Charlotte later adds that 'the house presented two pointed gables at its front', that 'the windows were latticed and narrow' and 'the front door was narrow, too, one step led up to it', we could be reading of many another large stone house along the border between Lancashire and Yorkshire. However these details do also fit Wycoller. Perhaps the best evidence that she might have had Wycoller in mind is that Ferndean is described as 'uninhabited' and 'unfurnished'. This is just how Wycoller would have looked through Charlotte's lifetime.

However even if we grant that Wycoller was indeed used within the novel, many features of the hall and the village are inconsistent with Ferndean and its surroundings. Charlotte makes no mention of the packhorse and other interesting early bridges or the curious vaccary walls which are such a feature of Wycoller Dene. Again Ferndean, hidden from the world in its 'forest' with no other houses within view conjures up a very different picture from that of Wycoller Hall, standing at the very heart of its once busy community. It is most significant of all that there is no mention of Wycoller's most famous feature, the huge fireplace. It seems that like Emily in *Wuthering Heights* Charlotte was prepared to use real landscapes and buildings; but again like her sister, she certainly did not feel bound to use these slavishly, but to use her gift for visual detail to blend various places and people she had seen into new forms to inhabit her novels.

THE WALK TO WYCOLLER HALL AND BOULSWORTH HILL

If arriving by bus, alight at the Hargreaves Arms between Colne and Keighley. Or if coming by car park on the section of old road on your left travelling from Colne about 300 yards beyond – east – of the Hargreaves Arms.

Assuming you have begun from the length of old road, walk down to the main road and turn right. Walk down taking great care until you are almost at the Hargreaves Arms. On your left you will see a gate and beside it if you look carefully a vandalised public footpath sign lying in the grass. Those who have come from the Hargreaves Arms will have crossed the road and walked left for a few yards. Cross the gate into the field. Walk parallel to the wall downhill until you come to a footbridge over the river Laneshaw. Cross the bridge and climb uphill to a stile. Over the stile walk in the general direction of the farm visible ahead. There is another stream to cross but it should present no problem. When you approach the farm aim for its right hand side into a corner of the field. If the stile is blocked you will find a gate just beyond it. Now turn right on the clear farm road and walk down to the main road.

At the road turn left for 20–30 yards then walk through the gate on the right hand side of the road. The right of way should now diverge half left from the lane down to the farm, pass through a field gate and turn right along the right hand field boundary to the bottom of the field, where you should cross a wall. This is blocked at the present time; I would suggest therefore that once through the gate into the farmyard you turn sharp right and walk alongside the lane you have just left until you come to a gate. Go through the gate and turn left and follow the wire fence on your left all the way down to the bottom of the field. Here turn left before some trees and then instantly right keeping the wall on your left. After about 50 yards look for a cluster of stiles on your left hand side. Cross over and walk in the general direction of the highest hills (Boulsworth Hill) ahead. Go through a stile by a gate and walk ahead along a broad grassy ledge to another stile next to a gate. Walk down the sandy track over the beck and turn left past some houses into the village.

You are now in the village of Wycoller, perhaps the most unspoilt village in the Brontë Country. The village has, however, altered greatly since the time of the Brontës. Many of the original cottages have been knocked down; several have been amalgamated to form one building, as in the case of Wycoller House; the old Methodist chapel has gone; an old cowshed has become a Craft Centre where one can also get good food. Above all what was essentially a busy working community has become, like so many others, a dormitory village.

Walk slowly through the village until you reach Wycoller Hall. If you have time do have a look round. Although Wycoller Hall goes back to at least the 17th century and probably well before, it was originally a fairly modest building with cottages clustered round it. It was the extravagant Henry Owen Cunliffe (1775–1818) who re-vamped the building to create the impression of a large ancient manor house. After his lifetime the hall was never again continuously occupied. In the time of the Brontës it would have slowly decayed from a complete but unoccupied building to an impressive ruin. Since the last decades of the 19th century it has frequently been associated with Ferndean Manor in *Jane Eyre*.

After surveying the hall, turn left along the track and follow it upstream with Wycoller Beck on your right. Pass the ancient slab bridge on the right. When the path forks at a plethora of footpath signs, climb over the stile and follow the stream on the right, Turnhole Clough, towards the right. Keeping within sight of this beck go up a rise to the right of a grassy hill and when you find the clear path at the top, walk

Boulsworth Hill from Barnside. This hill, the highest in the Brontë Country, is mentioned several times in Charlotte's early writings.

ahead to a footbridge. Cross the footbridge and turn left along a flagged path with a wooden fence and beck to the left. Go through a stile and keep alongside the wooden fence. After 150 yards cross a stile by a footbridge and turn right through a wood. The path is always clear, but if in doubt stay about 40 ft above the beck.

At the end of the wood climb a stile on the right and turn left with a wooden fence again to your left. Where the fence bends left down to the beck, walk ahead for a few yards and then follow the clear path half right downhill to a wooden stile. Over the stile climb some steps a few yards to the right and follow the now less distinct path ahead again keeping once again about 40 ft above the clough. A swampy patch is best passed on the right above. After resuming the path go over a stile by a gate to resume the Pendle Way, which you left at the bottom of Turnhole Clough.

Walk ahead towards the slopes of Boulsworth Hill. Climb uphill to join a wall on the right. Walk along for about ¾ mile. Go through a gate and continue ahead for a further

½ mile. Just after a stile on the right and before a deserted farm also on the right you will see a concrete road on the left leading uphill to a water treatment plant. This is the start of the permissive path up to Lad Law, the highest point of Boulsworth Hill. A rather indecipherable map by the side of the road gives details of the route. If you cannot work out the way from it, the following should hopefully be of some use. Turn up this concrete road until you reach the perimeter fence round the treatment plant. Go left round this fence following a broad green path waymarked from time to time with posts. Aim for a gate and kissing gate. Once through this keep in the same direction. If there is any discrepancy between the route indicated by the waymarks and the path, follow the path on the ground. When you finally reach the top of the surprisingly unrelenting climb, turn right by a tor which commands panoramic views both to north and south and walk for ⅓ mile to the obvious highest point of the ridge. The view is well worth the climb!

You are now at Lad Law – 'law' is a Saxon word for a hill – which is the highest point of the Boulsworth massif. The views from here can encompass much of Lancashire, York-shire and the south of Cumbria. The last day I was there I could see as far as Longridge Fell to the west, the Bowland Fells, the Lake District Fells, Pendle Hill, the Three Peaks, Buckden Pike, Great Whernside, Simon's Seat, Beamsley Beacon, Wolf Stones on Keighley Moor, Rombalds Moor, the Chevin, Withens Height, Stoodley Pike, Bleaklow and Hail Storm Hill in the Rossendale Hills.

After savouring the view leave the summit ridge and go half right following the waymarking posts downhill. Once again follow the clearest footpath. When you are nearing the bottom of the hill, aim for the corner of a stone wall below. When you reach the wall, walk straight ahead, keeping the wall on your right until you reach a large track, the Pendle Way, again. Turn right and follow this track until you pass a barn on the left and then a house. Turn left through a gate just beyond this house and, watching out for the none too friendly dog, walk ahead to another gate. Enter the field and walk ahead keeping parallel to the wall until you come to the low scattered remains of a wall coming in from the left and a stile with a post to the right. Cross the stile and walk half left, aiming a little to the left of a large grey farm ahead. When you reach a shallow dip in the field go down into it and follow it leftwards to a bridge over the stream in the bottom. Now walk straight ahead to three gates. Go through the one that is furthest right and walk ahead to another gate which takes you into a farmyard. Walk to the right of the farm and take the farm lane ahead. When you reach a metalled road continue to walk straight ahead.

Now follow this road for about ¼ mile. At the first farm lane on the right leave the road and walk up past two cottages. Here too there are dogs – very noisy dogs – but they should be secured. Once past the cottages turn left and then swing right uphill to the corner of a wall coming up from the left. From here head for a gate to the right of the farm ahead. Once through this gate go through a stile to the right of the gate on your right, turn left and head for the gate in the wire fence ahead. Through this aim for the house ahead. When you meet a wall turn left and then right at a corner and walk ahead to a stile. Walk left round the farm to join at its far side a farm lane. Turn left and walk ahead to a gate and stile. Continue in the same direction through this and again when you come to a crossroad of tracks. When the lane comes to an end continue with the fence on the right hand side. Cross over a stile and then again continue in the same direction with the fence still on the right. You should now encounter one of the rarities of the Wycoller Valley – a pulpit stile. Cross over this and keep ahead with a wall now on the right. Cross another stile and head for the corner of the coniferous wood visible ahead.

You are now privileged to cross another pulpit stile! Now enter the wood and follow the clear path through the trees, first of all along the right hand side of the wood and then through its middle. Cross the stile at the bottom and go down

The pack horse bridge at Wycoller.

to steps. Turn left down the stony track and follow it to the bottom. Keep left when it becomes a metalled road to retrace your steps through Wycoller.

You are now following the same route as you came by back to Barnside. Cross Wycoller Beck and then after a second bridge turn right along a track past some old houses. Now cross the beck for a third time and walk ahead to a gate and stile. Through the stile walk ahead to another gate and stile. Now walk ahead with a wall to your left. When you come to a wall ahead with a stile cross the wall and turn right keeping the wall on your right hand side. When you come to another wall you should really cross here and walk ahead up the field keeping the field boundary to your left until you come to a gate. Unless this is clear the best thing is to turn 10 yards left and then turn right to follow the right hand wire fence uphill. Go past the farm up to the top of the field. Here go through a gate and walk ahead to a track and a gate. Turn left through the gate on to a main road. Turn left for 20–30 yards and then turn right through a gate.

Follow the farm track uphill. Just before the farm turn left along a fence side and then turn right to a gate. Through the gate turn left and aim for a farm, Barnside, on the hillside ahead. Go down into a dip and climb out, still following the same direction. When you see a wall ahead follow it down to its bottom corner. Cross the stile and then the footbridge and then follow the wall on your right uphill to the gate and the main road. If you have parked your car on the old road above the Hargreaves Arms turn right and walk uphill. If you are going to catch the bus, why not enjoy some of the hospitality of the pub?

14

Edinburgh: Charlotte's 'Athens of the North'

Walking Distance: 3 miles

Our route links together most of the places Charlotte visited on her trip to Edinburgh. Starting from Waverley Bridge on the approximate site of the old General Station on Canal Street we visit and climb the Scott Monument for a commanding view of the city. We then saunter up into the Old Town, turn left to walk down the Royal Mile to Holyrood Park and climb the extinct volcano, Arthur's Seat, as Charlotte did. We return by Holyrood Palace itself and the Royal Mile.

Outside Yorkshire itself, only one place held the minds of all four young Brontës in thrall. This was Scotland. Three of the family's favourite writers were Scots – Hume, Burns and, most especially, Scott. Their favourite magazine, *Blackwood's*, was produced in Scotland. Its editor and many of its contributors were Scots and gave a specifically Scottish slant to the British and European issues that it discussed. As perhaps never before or since, Edinburgh was a sort of 'counter-capital' to London – 'The Athens of the North'.

It was not so surprising then that Scotland and things Scottish should have pervaded the children's writings. When they were small and each one had picked his own 'island', Emily had chosen Arran as her island, Scott as her 'cheif man' and Lockhart and Johnnie Lockhart as his companions. A little later Branwell went one better by producing his own 'Branwells Blackwoods Magazine'. In it he even wrote an extensive review of James Macpherson's *Ossian*. In 1834

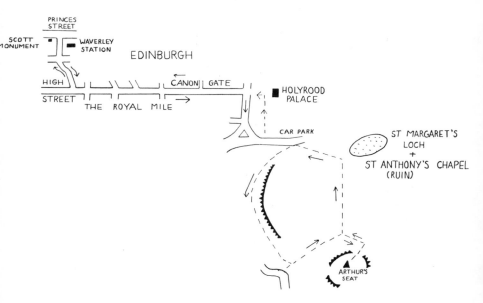

Charlotte, in response to an enquiry from Ellen, suggested that Hume, Burns, Scott and Lockhart were all writers whom she could read with profit. Letters sent by Branwell to *Blackwood's Magazine* seem to show that he knew great chunks of articles by 'Christopher North' off by heart. Not only that: throughout their creative lives all four children seem to have had at their fingertips a fund of Scots words, phrases, sayings, even complete poems that they deployed through their writings almost, it seems, at will.

But none of them actually seem to have tried to visit Scotland until almost the end. Obviously the problems and cost of coach and then rail travel did not help. Even when railway lines at last opened it remained both inconvenient and expensive to travel very far.

So how did Charlotte come to visit Edinburgh? It resulted from her choice of publisher. When Charlotte was still sending her first novel, *The Professor*, round – to the rascally Newby amongst others – only one of the publishers had the common decency to write her a proper reply. This was the relatively new firm of Smith, Elder and Co. As Charlotte herself wrote later: (The firm) 'declined, indeed, to publish that tale, for business reasons, but it discussed its merits and demerits so courteously, so considerately, in a spirit so rational, with a discrimination so enlightened, that this very refusal cheered the author better than a vulgarly-expressed acceptance would have done. It was added, that a work in three volumes would receive careful consideration.'

This work was, of course, to be *Jane Eyre*, which Charlotte, we are told by Mrs Gaskell, instantly set about writing on receipt of her last rejection. It must have pleased her that, by some coincidence, the publisher that had shown this interest was, like her beloved *Blackwood's*, Scots through and through. Both the original Smith and Elder came from the north east corner of Scotland. This was the first step then, but the friendship – and romance? – which were to lead Charlotte to visit Scotland might never have happened but for the unusual circumstances of publication. The Brontë sisters had published under *noms de plume*. Smith, Elder and Co had published Currer Bell; Ellis and Acton were published by Thomas Newby. Almost inevitably as the novels became best sellers, speculation began to run wild. It was realised that the name Bell was probably a pseudonym. Lockhart hypothesised that the 'Bells' were 'brothers of the weaving order in some Lancashire town'. *The Dublin University Magazine* surmised that 'the three personages were in reality but one'. Fashionable society was inclined to think that Currer Bell was a jilted mistress of Thackeray's who had got her own back on him by depicting him as Rochester. Even when the truth began to emerge and the puzzling name Brontë was bandied about, the overall consensus was that they must be relatives of Lord Nelson, Duke of Brontë.

In view of all this feverish gossip and Newby's attempts to suggest that the Bells were indeed only one person, Smith, Elder and Co demanded that the Bells acted to set the record straight. So in July 1848 it was decided that two of the Bells would have to visit London in person – Currer and Acton.

Holyrood Palace.

There was no chance, of course, that Ellis would agree.

Even in the stirring chronicle of the Brontës' lives this was an epic trip. First tea; then the journey down to Keighley 'through a snow-storm' (though it was July); then the train from Keighley into Leeds; then travelling overnight first class to London; the arrival at the Chapter Coffee House in time for breakfast; and then finally the walk to 65 Cornhill, the premises of Smith, Elder and Co, and the unexpected demand to see George Smith, the firm's young director.

'That particular Saturday' George Smith was to write over 30 years later, 'I was at work in my room when a clerk reported that two ladies wished to see me. I was very busy and sent out to ask their names. The clerk returned to say that the ladies declined to give their names but wished to see me on a private matter. After a moment's hesitation I told him to show them in. I was in the midst of my correspondence and my thoughts were far away from 'Currer Bell' and *Jane Eyre*. Two rather quaintly-dressed little ladies, pale-faced and anxious-looking walked into my room; one of them came forward and presented me with a letter, addressed, in my own handwriting, to 'Currer Bell Esq'. I noticed that the letter had been opened, and said, with some sharpness, 'Where did you get this from?' 'From the post-office,' was the reply; 'it was addressed to me. we have both come that you might have ocular proof that there are at least two of us.' This, then, was 'Currer Bell' in person.'

So it was that Charlotte met the man on whom she herself was to admit she based Doctor John Graham Bretton. For the first time in her life she, and briefly Anne, was swept up into the fashionable life of London, that life of which she had so fondly dreamed during her Verdopolis days. That very same evening George Smith hauled the two sisters off to the opera to see *The Barber of Seville*, an experience perhaps reflected in the visit to the opera in *Villette*. Next morning George Smith took them to that other fashionable meeting place, Wren's St Stephen's Wallbrook. On the following day they visited the Royal Academy and National Gallery, ate with Mr Smith and later at Mr Williams'. On the Tuesday they returned to Haworth.

This new connection could not have come at a more opportune time for Charlotte. The period that followed was to see the sickness and then the death of Branwell, Emily and Anne in horrifyingly quick succession. It seems certain that her new friends helped her to get through both the grief and the terrible depressions that followed on after that. And perhaps because of this desolation on Charlotte's side and George Smith's natural sensitivity and kindness, deeper bonds were forged than might have been expected.

The holiday in Scotland followed on almost automatically. First, however, came two prolonged stays with Mrs Smith and her son – the first from the 29 November to about 12 December 1849, the second from 30 May to 25 June 1850. Charlotte wrote to Ellen of the mixture of respect and alarm with which Mrs Smith initially regarded her, but how the distrust had slowly died away. In one respect, however, Mrs Smith was not to change. 'Mrs. Smith' Charlotte wrote, 'is

rather stern, but she has sense and discrimination; she
watched me very narrowly when surrounded by gentlemen,
she never took her eye from me. I like the surveillance both
when it kept guard over me amongst many, or only with her
cherished one.'

It was amidst such undercurrents that George suddenly
sprung on them all the idea of a trip to Scotland. As befitted a
family of Scottish origin, George's youngest brother was at
school in Scotland. One evening, completely without any
warning, George announced that he intended to take one of
his sisters with him to collect the boy and, as though by
afterthought, suggested 'Miss Brontë should join them there'.
Charlotte wrote that she had laughed and declined. George,
however, had pressed on seriously with the idea. It does not
need a Sherlock Holmes to see that the mention of the sister
first had been deliberately designed to forestall any objections
that it would be improper for Charlotte to go. There would
be a chaperone. At the start Mrs Smith had opposed the idea.
'You may easily fancy,' Charlotte wrote 'how she helped me
to sustain my opposition'. And this would, of course, have
made it impossible for her to go. George, however, was
serious and it seems clear he put pressure on his mother to
accede. Next morning Mrs Smith begged Charlotte to agree.
Under these circumstances she had little choice but to fall in
with the idea. With all that Scotland had meant to them – and
Emily perhaps most of all – she must have wanted to do so all
along.

She arranged to make the journey between two visits to
Ellen at Brookroyd. Perhaps she planned it in this way in
order to discuss the trip and its implications both before and
after the event. So it was that she arrived in Birstall on the 25
June, travelled to Edinburgh on 3 July, spent the 4th and 5th
in Scotland, returned to Brookroyd on the 6th and then
stayed there until 15 July.

Edinburgh, an even more beautiful city then than now, was
all that she had dreamed of and more. Afterwards she was to
write rapturously of 'Dun Edin', of 'mine own romantic

town', of 'Scott's monument' and Arthur's Seat. A lot of the time she was there she spent travelling, but there were no such complaints about being on the move all the time as there were to be when she visited Windermere a few weeks later. Far from that, Charlotte wrote that 'the enjoyment experienced in that little space equalled in degree and excelled in kind all which London yielded during a month's sojourn.'

It seems clear that George Smith had worked out a series of trips to places that would mean something to her. So it was that they drove out to Melrose and Abbotsford. 'We were fortunate' George Smith was to write many years later, 'in getting a driver, whom we engaged for the whole of our visit, who knew every interesting nook and corner in Edinburgh, who was better read in Scottish history and the Waverley Novels than I was, and whose dry humour exactly suited Miss Brontë.' However, the climax of the holiday was probably her ascent of Arthur's Seat following in the footsteps of the royal family and a picnic together at the summit. In a letter to James Taylor, the little man who was beginning to fall in love with her and some of whose traits are integrated into the character of Paul Emmanuel, she wrote 'I shall not soon forget how I felt when, having reached its summit, we all sat down and looked over the city, towards the sea and Leith, and the Pentland Hills.'

Even granted that she was writing to a Scot and was trying to propitiate him for having snubbed him earlier, she had plainly been very happy. However, as she had anticipated the trip was too much for her. When she got back to Brookroyd Ellen had to inform Mr Brontë that Charlotte was far from well. Alarmed equally at Charlotte's state of health and the prospect of a 'courtship' that would take his mainstay in life away from him, Mr Brontë worked himself up into such a state that when she got back to Haworth Charlotte found the stationer, Mr Greenwood, had been prevailed upon to set out in search of her. She was anything but pleased.

The slightly ambiguous relationship between Charlotte and George Smith was to continue through letters and her visits to London. A turning point in their relationship seems to have come with the publication of *Villette*. The picture she drew of George Smith and his mother as the Brettons was an affectionate one bathed in the same nostalgic glow as life at Gomersal in *Shirley*. The Smiths, however, recognising what Charlotte had done, were rather taken aback and a coolness set in between them. By late 1853 there was virtually no correspondence with George. When Charlotte heard of his engagement to Elizabeth Blakeway, she sent him a curt letter of congratulation –

'My dear Sir,
    In great happiness, as in great grief, words of sympathy should be few. Accept my need of congratulations – and believe me
                    Sincerely yours
                    Charlotte Brontë'

The dream that had begun at Edinburgh was at an end.

THE WALK AROUND EDINBURGH

Start at the Scott Monument just outside Waverley Station. Charlotte specifically mentions it in her letters. We cannot be certain whether she climbed it or not, but it is something not to be missed – probably at the start of the walk whilst you have plenty of energy. On descending, turn left and walk up to the main road (Waverley Bridge) and turn right to walk towards the Old Town. At the end of the bridge cross Market Street carefully and walk up Cockburn Street (pronounced 'Coh-burn'). At the top turn left into High Street, the Royal Mile. This is by far the most fascinating street in Edinburgh and much as it was in the time of Charlotte's visit.

    Cross North and South Bridge – again with great care – and continue down the street ahead, Canongate, passing as you do so an incredible wealth of ancient buildings, several of them now museums. As you will be returning this way it is probably best to leave exploring these in detail until your walk back. Informative maps and books on the Royal Mile can be purchased from several shops along the way. Walk past John Knox's House on the left and Huntly House on the right. Then a few yards after Canongate Church on the left turn right along Horse Wynd, for preference along the far (east) pavement. Follow this to the end, then turn left for about 50 yards and then right. When you reach the large car park cross the road, The Queen's Drive, again with exceptional care, into Holyrood Park. Make for the footpath which climbs to the right uphill *below* Salisbury Crags. As you ascend you will see superlative views of Edinburgh, the Firth of Forth and Fife beginning to unfold to the north. As you curve southeastwards the Southern Uplands too will come into view.

After a while the path gradually levels out and begins to descend. You will see a road ahead, once again The Queen's Drive. Keeping to the main track, descend towards this but before you reach it turn left up a rocky path which goes through a sort of pass in the hillside to your left. When you reach the top look out for two paths. Take the slightly indistinct one to the left which climbs the contours of the hill on your right very gradually. (Note: the path on the right which climbs straight uphill is dangerous!) Follow this as it contours its way gradually uphill then equally gradually loses height. Pass by two sets of wooden steps uphill on the right and also a path heading for two low crags below you on the left. Keep to the path ahead until you reach some wooden steps uphill on the main path itself. Climb these, curve gradually right across the slope and, still on the main path, go down an acute bend to the right. You now climb and contour your way above a shallow valley to your left. Follow the path as it heads towards a small notch on the skyline at the head of the valley ahead. When you reach this, turn right up the rocky slopes to the summit of Arthur's Seat. By now you will be definitely following in Charlotte's footsteps.

Stay as long at the top as temperature and inclination

Arthur's Seat, which Charlotte climbed with George Smith on her visit in 1850.

allow. Then retrace your steps to the notch. Here turn left and walk back down hill along the sides of the shallow valley – now to your right. At a fork turn right along a path which goes down the *left* hand side of the valley. Keep down this good path all the way to the bottom of the valley. When you see a ruined chapel, St Anthony's Chapel, on an outcrop over to the right and a small lake, St Margaret's Loch, below, also to the right, bear left and head along the path straight towards Holyrood Palace. Keep left and at roughly the same contour and eventually you will meet a metalled path.

Go right along this to meet at last the path by which you climbed Salisbury Crags. Cross the main road, The Queen's Drive, into the car park. Now turn left and walk round the perimeter of the palace grounds to the main gates. Go through the gates into the courtyard of the Palace. If you have time and the Palace is open it is well worth having a look round. Otherwise walk across the courtyard to the gate on the left and go through into Abbey Strand.

From here cross into Canongate, the Royal Mile, and make

your way back uphill over the bridges to Cockburn Street on the right. Turn down this and in a few minutes you will be back at the Scott Monument on Prince's Street. As you make this return journey you will pass almost innumerable buildings of first rate historical and architectural importance, not to mention many good eating places and excellent pubs, and it would seem a shame not to explore some of these, if you have sufficient time. Why not buy a map or guide to the Royal Mile, sit down at leisure and work out how to make the best of your return journey?

15

Charlotte's Lakeland: Jenkin Crag, Troutbeck, Wansfell Pike and Lake Windermere

Walking Distance: 8 miles

We begin from Ambleside, a town Charlotte must have visited several times on her sojourns in the Lakes. Charlotte would have been driven around the area so her routes would not be suitable for modern walkers. We have taken a route which visits or surveys the main places rather than follows Charlotte's itineraries exactly. We begin by walking up Jenkin Crag with its panoramic view of Windermere and then descend to Lowood where Charlotte went boating with Sir James Kay-Shuttleworth and Mrs Gaskell. We then climb by footpath up to Briery Close where they were all staying. From here we walk to Troutbeck, a village she possibly visited, and then return over Wansfell Pike. This may have been one of the fells that Charlotte wished she could have explored on her own. The stunning view from the summit encompasses pretty well the whole of Charlotte's Lakeland.

The Windermere area meant something more in the Brontës' time than now. It was not just fine scenery. There was a concentration of intellectuals there that would have been impossible to encounter outside London, including Wordsworth, Southey, Coleridge and De Quincey.

It is not then surprising that it was primarily as an intellectual centre that the Lakes were to figure in the Brontës' lives. The young Brontës' first attempts to contact Lakes intellectuals were unsuccessful. Although they made valiant efforts,

the family were, it seemed, to be disappointed in their efforts
to interest the Lakes intelligentsia in themselves.

However, by some quirk of fate it was to be in the Lakes
that Charlotte was to establish just such a link as those of
which she had dreamed. It was to happen in a fairy tale sort
of way through Sir James Kay-Shuttleworth of Gawthorpe
Hall, Padiham. *Shirley* was published on 26 October 1849 –
still under the *nom de plume* of Currer Bell. The news that
Charlotte was Currer Bell only came out in Haworth on 4
February 1850. By January Sir James, who had probably
learnt the truth in London, had already written to Charlotte
congratulating her on *Shirley*, desiring to make her acquaintance and inviting her over to Gawthorpe. By March he had
written again and driven over to Haworth to beard 'the
literary lion' in her den and, hopefully to bear her away.

The ploy did not work, though, as part of the price for not
leaving at once, Charlotte had to agree to spend three days at
Gawthorpe a few days later. What followed became a tragi-
comic tug of war between Charlotte and the Kay-

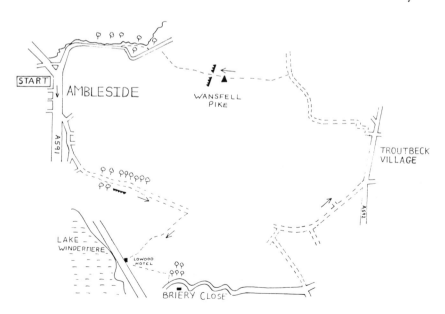

Briery Close where Charlotte met some of the Lakeland Intelligentsia on her visit to friends. She was also to be first acquainted with Mrs Gaskell there.

Shuttleworths. They wanted Charlotte to accompany them to London for the Season. She was as determined not to go. Finally after postponements due to the sickness of Mr Brontë and then Sir James himself, it was agreed that Charlotte should visit the Kay-Shuttleworths at Briery Close, the house which he had rented above Windermere, on Sunday 18 August.

The train journey was a slow and awkward one with changes at Skipton and Lancaster. At Lancaster she had to wait around for an hour and a half before she could catch her connection to Windermere. However she was met at last by Sir James at Windermere station – at 8 pm – and driven through the fading light along the road to Ambleside and then up the steep climb to Briery Close itself. She wrote her impressions to her father next morning:

'The place is exquisitely beautiful, though the weather is cloudy, misty and stormy; but the sun bursts out occasionally and shows the hills and the lake.'

Beyond the beauty of the scenery and Briery Close itself, 'a pretty house', according to Mrs Gaskell, built in Westmorland stone with views across Windermere to the southern fells, the visit was only a mixed success. Charlotte found the Kay-Shuttleworths 'kind', Sir James himself, as an earlier letter tells us, 'gracious and dignified' and his wife full of 'frankness, goodhumour and activity'. But there was an obvious clash between his 'practical' attitudes and her own 'vagrant' instincts. It seems apparent each said and did things which grated a little on the others. However even Charlotte conceded there was an 'artistic' side to Sir James as well as his 'wordly' and 'utilitarian' one. And as part and parcel of this and a genuine affection for Charlotte he was anxious to introduce her to other leading literary figures. By far the most important of these was to be Mrs Gaskell. Sir James had invited Mrs Gaskell to come up to Windermere on Tuesday August 20 and after a longish journey, Mrs Gaskell arrived in the dark. For once we have first hand evidence of the event:

'A little lady in a black silk gown ... she came up and shook hands with me at once. I went up to unbonnet etc., came down to tea, the little lady worked away and hardly spoke; but I had time for a good look at her. She is ... undeveloped; thin and more than a head shorter than I, soft brown hair not so dark as mine; eyes (very good and expressive looking straight and open at you) of the same colour, a reddish face; large mouth and many teeth gone; altogether *plain*, the forehead square, broad and *rather* overhanging. She has a very sweet voice.'

No less interestingly she gives some insight into the routines at Briery Close mostly devised by Sir James himself, since Lady Kay-Shuttleworth was 'indisposed'. After Mrs Gaskell had made the breakfast their first visitor appeared, to have breakfast with them, a Mr Moseley, Inspector of Schools. After breakfast, the four of them had gone boating on the lake (presumably at Low Wood). Perhaps on the same day, after lunch, Sir James decided to run them over to Fleet Lodge, Coniston, to meet the Tennysons. Thoughtfully he let the ladies ride inside, whilst he rode outside on the box. However it began to rain and the party turned back.

Next day the trip was more successful. Sir James had arranged in advance for all three of them to be invited to tea at Fox How near Ambleside to meet the widow and children of Dr Arnold. Charlotte in her usual amazingly graphic way sums the scene up for us:

'It was twilight as I drove to the place. The house looked like a nest half buried in flowers and creepers: and, dusk as it was, I could feel that the valley and the hills round were beautiful as imagination could dream.'

Here too the introductions went on. Charlotte and party met not just Mrs Arnold and her daughters but the son of Bunsen, the Prussian Ambassador, and his wife. She was now actually living out the dreams she had committed to paper in her juvenilia.

Even on her last day at Briery Close, she was to meet more visitors. Mrs Ferrand the wife of the former Conservative MP for Knaresborough, who owned St Ives, a large mansion close to Haworth, came over to pay her respects together with Lord John Manners, who brought over a brace of grouse for Mr Brontë. Both were Conservatives, unlike the Kay-Shuttleworths; both were associated with Disraeli and his Young England movement. However, all this fêting had its negative side: not for the first time and not for the last Charlotte developed one of her nervous headaches. Perceptive as ever, Mrs Gaskell noticed how 'taxed' her nerves were by the effort of going amongst strangers. And no less truthful herself, Charlotte confided in a letter to Miss Wooler that she had only been 'half at her ease' and how much more she would have preferred to get out of the carriage and run away by herself amongst the hills and dales.

In spite of these unsatisfactory aspects, the visit was to be one of major importance. For the first time for many years she had made a new close sympathetic friend, Mrs Gaskell, who with her Dissenting Christianity and Liberal views, perhaps helped fill the yawning gap left by Mary Taylor. In

The view of Lake Windermere from Briery Close.

the visits the two great women writers paid to each other in April and September 1853, it is plain Mrs Gaskell became the sort of confidante her two dead sisters had been. The fleeting visit to Briery Close led not just to *The Life of Charlotte Brontë,* one of the greatest biographies in English, but to two friendships destined to be of great value during what was left of Charlotte's life and in the period that followed. For it was due to Sir James and Mrs Gaskell acting in concert that the earliest of her mature novels – and the last to be published – was to see the light of day. It was in consequence of yet another visit by Sir James – this time with Mrs Gaskell – that Mr Nicholls finally and very reluctantly released the manuscripts of *The Professor,* the uncompleted *Emma* and some of the juvenilia. As earlier, Sir James had steamrollered his way over others' objections to get what he wanted. Mrs Gaskell thought it was largely because he wished to get part of the glory himself, but this is probably too cynical.

The visit to Briery Close was certainly the most important visit to the Lakes. However, Charlotte was to return. In

December 1849 she had contacted Harriet Martineau, who was on a visit to London, and paid her a call. Twelve months later Harriet Martineau invited her over for a week to her house, The Knoll at Ambleside.

Whilst in Ambleside, she dined out at the house of Wordsworth's son-in-law, Edward Quillinan. On Saturday 21 December she visited Mrs Arnold again at Fox How, where she met Matthew Arnold. Neither on first acquaintance was very impressed with the other. However, apart from the introductions and conversations it must be said that the main effect of her visits to the Lakes was a negative one. There was never to be any poetic or prose celebration of either the scenery or the way of life there. The glittering company of which she had so fondly dreamed proved to be an ordeal; the ideas they put forward repelled and disturbed her. It seems no accident that on her return from Harriet Martineau's she went straight to Brookroyd to spend Christmas with her oldest, closest and most reassuring friend, Ellen.

THE WALK TO TROUTBECK AND WANSFELL PIKE

Park where possible in Ambleside. Then start in the middle of the town outside the National Trust property, Bridge House. With your back to the house turn right and follow the main road, the A591 past the Salutation Hotel on the far side of the road as it curves round to become Lake Road. Follow this for about 300 yards to Kelsick Road, then cross the road and walk up Old Lake Road, which runs parallel to, but above Lake Road itself. Where Low Gale and Blue Hill Road branch off uphill to the left keep straight along Old Lake Road walking along the back of a series of large slate-built and whitewashed houses.

Keep straight on past Fisherbeck Lane and past the car park to the right and then turn half left up Skelghyll Lane. There is a signpost just visible to the left of the lane bearing the words 'Jenkins Crag (sic), Skelghyll and Troutbeck

(Bridleway)'. As you climb this narrow lane, views over the head of Lake Windermere and the northern end of the Coniston Fells open up. The lane climbs steadily uphill past a number of large houses until at a sign saying 'Jenkyn's Crag' (sic) and another one saying 'Broad Ings' you fork right. After about 300 yards there is another fork. This time the Broad Ings sign points left. Here you should fork right.

From this point onwards the old lane is rougher underfoot. By now the views extend round as far as the two Langdale valleys. Keep right at yet another fork (the left hand track leads to Skelgarth). Keep left of the National Trust sign at the start of Skelghyll Woods but right at the gateway saying 'Skelghyll Woods Private'. One hundred yards further on fork left following the National Trust sign pointing to Jenkin Crag and Troutbeck.

The track is rougher still now. There is a chicken wire fence to the left and a small wooded ravine to the right. At yet another fork, curve right over a bridge. There is a slate as you approach it bearing the words 'Jenkin Crag Skelghyll Troutbeck'. Then 30 yards past the bridge, fork left and zigzag up through the woods until you meet a dry stone wall on the right. Follow this until you meet a gap in this wall and a National Trust sign saying 'Jenkyn's Crag'. Go through this gap and walk the few yards to the crag itself. From the top of the rocks – and the best view is from the furthest one – a fine panorama opens up which includes much of Lake Windermere, the woods on the far side, Wray Castle, the Coniston Fells and the Langdale Pikes.

After you have had your fill of this magnificent vista, retrace your steps to the gap in the wall and turn right along the track. This continues to run roughly parallel – or sometimes close up – to the wall and later on wire fence on the right. As you leave the woods there are yet more views of Lake Windermere and the cluster of islands in the middle. When you reach a gate, go through it and continue with the wire fence to the right. Now pass through another gate marked 'To Troutbeck', into a farmyard. Keep to the right hand side of the farm and then between two buildings to emerge onto a metalled road.

Follow this road for about 300 yards, then just before a bridge turn right off the metalled road on to a rough track which runs downhill roughly parallel to an oakwood and a stream. Pass through a gate and continue along the track which now veers right to meet a stone wall. Keep this on the right for about 100 yards then turn right over a stile and follow another wall, this time on the left, for another 100 yards to another stile. Cross this and then go across the field aiming roughly in the direction of Wray Castle, whose battlements should be visible among the trees on the far side of the lake. You will soon see yet another wall with a ladder-stile across it. Climb over this and walk down the field ahead keeping close to the wall on the right. When you are nearly at the bottom of the field, strike left to a kissing gate to the left of a wooden gate. Once through again go down the field close to the wall on the right until at the bottom of the field you will find another kissing gate. Go through this and walk between the buildings of the Low Wood Hotel out to the main road.

Turn left for a few yards in front of the hotel and cross the road into a green enclosure for a view of the lake. This is certainly a view which Charlotte would have enjoyed as she went boating or for drives with Sir James and Lady Kay-Shuttleworth. Here it is possible to take the bus back to Ambleside or if you wish to omit the first part of the walk, to join the second half.

After surveying the lake, cross the road again, turn left in front of the hotel and walk back to the lane between the buildings on the right. Turn right and climb up to the kissing gate. There should be two footpath signs. This time take the one pointing half right. The path is not always clear. To start with there will be a wire fence a few yards away to the right. When that bends away to the right continue straight ahead towards some woods. The path is now just about visible as a depression in the field. As you approach the woods you will see a metal kissing gate roughly 75 yards to the right of the left hand edge of the woods. Go through this gate and follow the pebbly path left and over a stone footbridge. Once over this turn right, cross a more ramshackle bridge and then climb by the broad track to the right up through the woods to a metalled road. Turn left. The large impressive complex of buildings ahead and to the right is Briery Close where Charlotte stayed with Sir James and Lady Kay-Shuttleworth and met Mrs Gaskell. You will see it first across a field and then pass by its gates, but the property itself is strictly private.

After passing Briery Close, walk for almost ¾ mile. Pass by a public footpath sign on the left and when you come to a farm and a barn on the right look out for a footpath sign on the left to the left hand side of a stony lane. Follow this lane uphill between its fences and walls until you reach a stile. Cross this and then make your way up the rather rough, rutted ground ahead to another stile to the left hand side of a gate. If in doubt keep close to the wall on the right. Cross this second stile into a lane, turn right and a few yards later turn right again along another lane. You should now command an extensive view across the length of Windermere and its islands.

Now follow this lane, deviating neither to left nor right as it slowly curves round left into the Troutbeck Valley. As you proceed downhill the fine southern end of the High Street range will become increasingly visible ahead. You pass by a few old houses on the left and then you join a main road at Troutbeck Post Office. It is often possible to buy light refreshments here.

On joining the main road, turn left and follow this road through the well spaced out houses of the village for about ½ mile until you reach a footpath sign on the right hand side of the road opposite to Lane Foot Farm and marking the route to Wansfell. Turn left here between the farm and barn, pass through a gate and climb up the track between the walls as it zigzags its way uphill. There are no problems during this section of the walk – except, perhaps, for the steepness of the

Troutbeck Village; one of the villages which Charlotte possibly visited with Sir James Kay-Shuttleworth and Mrs Gaskell.

climb itself. All the time there are fine views across to Froswick and Ill Bell. After about 1½ miles of steady climbing go through the gate on the left. There is a sign saying 'Footpath to Ambleside'. Now follow the clear path across the enclosed fell-land to another gate in the wall ahead and then follow the clear path as it winds first a little to the right and then to the left to the curious wooden rails on the skyline. Once you reach these, the summit of Wansfell Pike is just a few more yards ahead through a stile. Here take a well-deserved rest.

There is an outstanding view in almost every direction. Ahead and to the left you can see virtually the whole of the Lake District visited by Charlotte spread out below. Working round in a circle from the Ambleside side you can see the Coniston range, the Langdale Pikes, the Thirlmere Fells, Stony Cove Pike and High Street.

After resting for a while admiring the views, follow the clear path round to the left of the small knob of rock ahead and then down the obvious route. This part is steep and requires some care. Then follow the all too clear footpath down the steep slope into the valley. Many of the stones are loose here and again require some care. However, there is no more difficulty than one finds on most Lake District paths. Provided one takes the route at a speed appropriate to one's age and sense of balance there should be no serious problems.

At the bottom you will come to a green lane and then a ladder stile. Cross both and then follow the clear path first of all straight ahead and then half left a few yards to the left of a barbed wire fence. Follow this fence round to a stile and beyond the stile a metal ladder which will take you down to the road below. Turn left along the road and walk down it for 200 yards, looking out on the right for an unusual old-fashioned turnstile leading into some woods. Pass through this and go right into the woods until you come to a picnic table and benches. Here turn left and follow the path, forking left again when this path divides just after some steps. Now follow the path steadily downhill through the woods until you see a gate ahead and a gap leading out into a road. Turn right on this road and walk down hill. At the bottom turn right by the public conveniences and go straight ahead past the Salutation Hotel on the right. In a few moments you will be back at the House on the Bridge, where the walk began.

Acknowledgements

I should like to thank the following for all the help they have given me during the course of writing this book:

Derek Bridge and the staff of the Calderdale Library

Stewart Cardwell and Irene Parker of Keighley
    Reference Library

Ian Dewhirst of Keighley

Helier Hibbs of Little Ouseburn, York

Hugh Murray of York

John Nussey of Chester

Barbara White of Murton, York

The Staff of the Brontë Parsonage Museum, Oakwell Hall, the Red House at Gomersall, Shibden Hall near Halifax and countless people of whom I have made enquiries when doing the 'fieldwork' for this book.

Bibliography

The Brontë Novels
All the Brontë novels are available relatively inexpensively in the Penguin Classics. The most authoritative edition is the Clarendon Edition, Oxford University Press.

Poetry
[Juliet Barker (ed)] The Brontës: *Selected Poems* (Dent 1985) carries a selection from all four Brontë children. There are some good notes, but it is, inevitably, incomplete.

[Janet Gezari (ed)] Emily Jane Brontë: *The Complete Poems* (Penguin 1992) is both inexpensive *and* scholarly.

Edward Chitham, Victor Neufeldt and Tom Winnifrith have all produced collections of poems by the individual Brontës over the last 20 years. These are all somewhat costly, but obviously more complete than an anthology.

Miscellaneous Writings
Selections of the juvenilia have appeared in several guides over the years.

[F. S. Beer (ed)] Jane Austen and Charlotte Brontë: *Juvenilia* (Penguin 1986)

Christine Alexander is also producing a definitive edition of the *Early Writings of Charlotte Brontë* in several volumes. For Branwell, Mary Butterfield has produced *Brother in the Shadows: Stories and Sketches by Branwell Brontë* (Bradford Libraries and Information Service 1988).

Letters
The 'standard' edition is T. J. Wise and J. A. Symington (eds) *The Brontës: Their Lives, Friendships and Correspondence in Four Volumes* (Blackwell 1932). There is also a pleasant selection by Muriel Spark available and Margaret Smith is working on a new, more accurate edition of Charlotte's letters.

Reference Works
B. and G. Lloyd Evans: *Everyman's Companion to the Brontës* (Dent 1982)

F. B. Pinion: *A Brontë Companion* (Macmillan 1975)

Lives
Elizabeth Gaskell: *The Life of Charlotte Brontë* (Penguin 1975). This edition contains not only the text of the controversial First Edition but also Mrs Gaskell's timid second thoughts. This remains the authoritative work on the Brontës. The only other biography by someone who knew a member of the family at first hand is Francis Leyland, *The Brontë Family* (Hurst and Blackett 1886). There are also good recent biographies by

Edward Chitham, Daphne du Maurier, Rebecca Fraser, Winifred Gérin, Annette B. Hopkins, John Lock and W. T. Dixon, and many others.

The Brontë Country
Phyllis Whitehead: *The Brontës Came Here* (Privately Printed, no date)
Herbert E. Wroot: *Persons and Places* (Brontë Society 1935)